D0349362

CONSTITUTIONAL RESTRICTIONS AGAINST STATE DEBT

CONSTITUTIONAL
RESTRICTIONS
AGAINST STATE DEBT

A. James Heins

HJ
8224
H45

THE UNIVERSITY OF WISCONSIN PRESS · *Madison* 1963

Published by
THE UNIVERSITY OF WISCONSIN PRESS
430 Sterling Court, Madison 6, Wisconsin

Copyright © 1963, by the
Regents of the University of Wisconsin

Printed in the United States of America
by George Banta Company, Inc., Menasha, Wisconsin

Library of Congress Catalog Number 63-9062

Preface

To BORROW or not to borrow is no longer the question. At one time, however, a study of constitutional restrictions against state debt would have been primarily concerned with that question. In 1900, a program of public works to be financed by state borrowing would have required constitutional revision in many states. A study engendered by this problem would have centered around the expected benefits of borrowing over taxation as compared with the possibility of debt mismanagement. Since 1900, however, states have developed means of borrowing for public improvements that escape constitutional bans. Courts in constitutionally restricted states have ruled that constitutional prohibitions do not apply to debts created through specific types of debt instruments. This development has been so complete that most states are now able to borrow funds in any amount for nearly any purpose.

While questions about the propriety of public borrowing are still important, they have limited applicability to problems created by the existence of constitutional debt restrictions in the states. Merely deciding that borrowing is a proper instrument of state finance would not be a compelling reason to abolish debt limitations, because states already have the means of borrowing. On the other hand, deciding that public borrowing is an improper instrument of state finance would not compel the retention of present restrictions, because they do not effectively restrict. The importance of constitutional debt restrictions lies in the impact their existence has on the options available to state officials in the

v

selection of a program of state debt for public improvements.

Constitutional prohibitions against state debt were born out of the financial difficulties encountered by numerous states prior to 1845. Caught by the depression of 1837 in an overextended debt position, nine states defaulted on their debt. Public revulsion in many states forced the adoption of constitutional amendments that prohibited future borrowing by state legislatures for works of internal improvement. In some states, the prohibition was mitigated by the inclusion of a referendum provision which permitted the electorate to approve borrowing for specific purposes; but in other states the restriction was absolute. Without exception, states joining the Union after 1845 wrote some form of debt restriction into their constitutions.

After 1900, mounting pressure to provide public improvements led some state legislatures to search for means of borrowing which would bypass constitutional restrictions. This search led to the development of revenue bonds, public corporations, lease-purchase agreements, and reimbursement obligations—devices which have enabled states to borrow funds without creating debt in the eyes of constitutional provisions. State debt created by these devices may be termed nonguaranteed debt in the sense that states do not pledge their general funds for the repayment of such debt. These nonguaranteed borrowing methods have become so refined that today most states can incur debt in any amount for virtually any purpose.

The development of nonguaranteed borrowing methods has not been without consequence, however. Because constitutional restrictions preclude a pledge of state credit or state taxing power to the repayment of nonguaranteed obligations, states must pay higher interest rates on this type of obligation. In order to bypass constitutional debt restrictions, states have had to create special administrative organizations, which all too often function inefficiently. In essence, restricted states are now able to borrow, but not without paying a premium for the privilege. This premium has led to a movement in some states to revise constitutional debt provisions to permit a pledge of state credit. Opponents of constitutional revision generally claim that, while borrowing is clearly not prevented, present restrictions significantly impede the growth of state debt. To these opponents of revision, the cost premium is of small significance when compared with the barrier that constitutional debt restrictions place against an overextended state debt.

I have concluded, however, that it is in the public interest to restore full borrowing power to state legislatures, with no referendum provisions, nor any other restriction commonly found in state constitutions. This conclusion was reached on the basis of the following observations:

1. State constitutions do not effectively restrict state legislatures as to the amount or purpose of state borrowing. The only real restrictions on the amount of state borrowing are the moral and political obligations of state legislators, which would exist in the absence of constitutional provisions.

2. Present restrictions reduce the number of options available to state legislatures in the planning of a sound debt policy. If borrowing is to be done in restricted states without costly referendums or constitutional amendments, it must be done via one of the nonguaranteed methods.

3. Nonguaranteed borrowing involves higher interest costs because of the greater risk lenders assume. To the extent that states intend repaying such loans regardless of the outcome of the project for which the funds were borrowed, but which because of constitutional restrictions are unable to make this intention known to lenders, the higher interest cost reflects a fictitious shift of risk from the public to the lenders, and hence becomes a real cost to the public.

4. The administrative procedures required to satisfy the courts that nonguaranteed borrowing is not state debt are often more costly than comparable administration of full-faith and credit debt.

5. State debt restrictions lead to the practice of interagency lending of state funds. This practice tends to understate the cost of state projects and results in an inequitable use of funds contributed by members of state retirement programs.

A study of this nature is only as good as the data that go into its making. In that light I thank Frank Morris of the Investment Bankers Association of America, Lynden Mannen and Jacob

Jaffe of the Census Bureau, Ray Rothermel of the Wisconsin Building Commission, and Page Ingraham of the Council of State Governments for helping me acquire the necessary data. A special note of thanks goes to the Tax Foundation for eliminating much legwork by allowing me to use portions of their Project Note No. 35, and to the many officers of state authorities who answered my letters and questionnaires.

James Earley, Robert Lampman, Harold Groves, and Donald Farrar read my preliminary manuscript and made many helpful suggestions. Gilbert Whitaker and William Bryan were especially helpful by showing me the ins and outs of the IBM 650. To all of them I express my gratitude and, rather reluctantly, absolve them of responsibility for any shortcomings which may follow.

Lastly, I thank my wife and children for bearing up under this project; and they have duly thanked me for finally getting it done.

A. JAMES HEINS

September 1962
University of Illinois
Urbana, Illinois

Contents

List of Tables

CONSTITUTIONAL RESTRICTIONS AGAINST STATE DEBT

1

The Origin and Development of State Debt Limits

T HE ORIGINAL thirteen states and the states admitted to the Union prior to 1840 were not constitutionally restricted in matters of state debt. The power of sovereign political units to borrow freely had long been established and most state constitutions did not refer to state borrowing. Prior to 1820 state debt largely consisted of short-term paper issued to meet operating deficits and the costs of conducting wars. While states did encounter financial difficulties in the wake of borrowing to finance the Revolution and the War of 1812, the federal government twice bailed out states in trouble by assuming their debts.[1] Subsequent to the War of 1812, the federal government assumed virtually the entire responsibility for the conduct of wars and, with a few exceptions during the Civil War, states have not borrowed for purposes of defense.

After 1817, however, states began programs of public borrowing to finance works of internal improvement. It was the overextension of this program that resulted in financial difficulties for many states and led to the eventual adoption of constitutional restrictions against state borrowing.

Borrowing for Works of Internal Improvement

Borrowing for public works as we know them today began in 1817 with New York's construction of the Erie Canal. When completed in 1825, the canal proved to be an immediate success. Freight traffic enabled revenue to exceed interest cost before the canal was completed. Prices of inland agricultural commodities

3

immediately increased, a sufficient demonstration to other states of the value of adequate transportation.[2]

The economic situation west of the Appalachians and in the Mississippi Valley was a perfect setting for the boom in state-financed transportation that followed. For many years the fertile farm land of the Midwest had been hampered by lack of access to Eastern and foreign markets. The introduction of the steamboat on the Mississippi River enabled many Midwestern farmers to find better markets, but people situated any distance from adequate river ports continued to face the problem of inadequate markets. To many of these people the success of the Erie Canal promised the answer to their economic problems. Within five years after the Erie Canal was completed, Pennsylvania, Maryland, and Ohio had borrowed money for canal construction.

Ohio began construction of a canal system connecting Lake Erie to the Ohio River. Pennsylvania, anxious for Philadelphia to meet the challenge of New York as the metropolis of the East, began an ambitious program of transportation improvements. Maryland followed suit for Baltimore with the Chesapeake and Ohio Canal and soon with the Chesapeake and Ohio Railroad.

In the Mississippi Valley, Indiana with the Wabash and Erie Canal, and Illinois with the Illinois and Michigan Canal, began the headlong rush for improvements which would enable them to compete in Eastern markets. Indiana borrowed $10 million in 1836 and Illinois $8 million in 1837 for grandiose systems of canals and railroads. Michigan followed with a loan of $5 million for improvements, although the total assessed value of property within the state amounted to less than $43 million—an ambitious undertaking for a small state.[3] Within ten years these three states were to default on their obligations.

Table 1 shows the growth of state debts from 1820 to 1841. Whereas state borrowing from 1820 to 1835 aggregated less than $68 million, the three-year period following 1835 witnessed new state issues in excess of $107 million, almost 60 per cent more than in the preceding fifteen-year period. These figures indicate the obsession of states with rapid economic development through state financed improvements.

TABLE 1

State borrowing, 1820–1841
(thousands of dollars)

State	Amount borrowed					Debt outstanding 1841
	1820–25	1825–30	1830–35	1835–38	Total	
Ala.	$ 100	$ —	$ 2,200	$ 8,500	$10,800	$15,400
Ark.	—	—	—	3,000	3,000	2,676
Fla.	—	—	1,500	—	—	4,000
Ga.	—	—	—	—	—	1,300
Ill.	—	—	600	11,000	11,600	13,527
Ind.	—	—	1,890	10,000	11,890	12,751
Ky.	—	—	—	7,369	7,369	3,085
La.	1,800	—	7,335	14,000	23,135	23,985
Me.	—	—	555	—	555	1,735
Md.	58	577	4,210	6,648	11,493	15,215
Mass.	—	—	—	4,290	4,290	5,424
Mich.	—	—	—	5,340	5,340	5,611
Miss.	—	—	2,000	5,000	7,000	7,000
Mo.	—	—	—	2,500	2,500	842
N.Y.	6,873	1,624	2,205	12,229	22,931	21,797
Ohio	—	4,400	1,701	—	6,101	10,924
Pa.	1,680	6,300	16,130	3,167	27,277	36,336
S.C.	1,250	310	—	4,000	5,560	3,691
Tenn.	—	—	500	6,648	7,148	3,398
Va.	1,030	469	686	4,133	6,318	4,037
Wis.	—	—	—	—	—	200
Totals	$12,791	$13,680	$41,513	$107,824	$174,307	$192,945

Source: Ratchford, *American State Debts* (1941), p. 79.

Other State Borrowing

In Southern states, the growth of state debt reflected another public demand: the enlargement of banking facilities. In the face of seemingly restricted short-term credit facilities, Southern states were urged to finance banking institutions, and they responded by chartering land banks, issuing state bonds to supply working capital. After the demise of the Second United States Bank in 1836, Southern states had a ripe excuse for carrying out their banking activities. By 1838 state debt incurred for banking purposes exceeded $54 million, most of it in states south of the Ohio River.[4] Table 2 gives a breakdown of state debt outstanding in 1838 by the purposes for which it was issued.

Sources of Funds

Because private capital was scarce in North America, the main outlet for state securities was in the European market. European investors eagerly purchased the security issues of the states for a variety of reasons. Because of the relative scarcity of capital in the United States, interest rates were generally higher than in Europe. The favorable credit rating established by the First and Second United States banks and by the United States government lent an aura of safety to American enterprise. The English in particular

TABLE 2

State debts outstanding in 1838 and purposes for which they were contracted
(thousands of dollars)

State	Banking	Canals	Railroads	Turn-pikes	Miscel-laneous	Total
Ala.	$ 7,800	$ —	$ 3,000	$ —	$ —	$ 10,800
Ark.	3,000	—	—	—	—	3,000
Fla.	1,500	—	—	—	—	1,500
Ill.	3,000	900	7,400	—	300	11,600
Ind.	1,390	6,750	2,600	1,150	—	11,890
Ky.	2,000	2,619	350	2,400	—	7,369
La.	22,950	50	500	—	235	23,735
Me.	—	—	—	—	555	555
Md.	—	5,700	5,500	—	293	11,493
Mass.	—	—	4,290	—	—	4,290
Mich.	—	2,500	2,620	—	220	5,340
Miss.	7,000	—	—	—	—	7,000
Mo.	2,500	—	—	—	—	2,500
N.Y.	—	13,317	3,788	—	1,158	18,262
Ohio	—	6,101	—	—	—	6,101
Pa.	—	16,580	4,964	2,596	3,167	27,307
S.C.	—	1,550	2,000	—	2,204	5,754
Tenn.	3,000	300	3,730	118	—	7,148
Va.	—	3,835	2,129	355	343	6,662
Totals	$54,140	$60,202	$42,871	$6,619	$8,475	$172,306

Source: Ratchford, *American State Debts*, p. 88.

apparently visualized the same rewards for public improvements that Americans saw, and they were anxious to invest in self-liquidating projects instead of in the war machines so common in Europe. By 1839 British investors held between $110 and $165 million in American securities.[5]

Banking and investment houses in the East with European outlets handled the bulk of the state security issues. Among these houses were the Second United States Bank, August Belmont, and Prime Ward and Company. Belmont and Prime Ward were the respective agents of the Rothschilds and Baring Brothers, the largest financial houses in Europe.

The Depression of 1837 and the Collapse of State Finances

Much has been written about the causes of the 1837 depression,[6] but all that will be said on this subject is that the rapid rise in state borrowing for unsuccessful internal improvements was undoubtedly a contributing factor. The severe panic of 1837 did not lead to an immediate reduction in state borrowing for several reasons. Many states had incomplete projects on their hands that had to be completed before revenues which would service the debt incurred for the projects could be realized. This fact, coupled with a general feeling that the recession was temporary and that business was "fundamentally sound," encouraged states to go ahead with their building programs.

The later collapse in 1839 and 1840 signaled the seriousness of the economic depression, and most state building programs came to a halt. States were beset by the problems of decreasing revenues due to the depression and mounting debt service requirements. Many canals and railroads constructed in this period were never completed and failed to provide any revenues, but nonetheless the debts had to be serviced. States were further hindered in their attempts to meet their debts by a general deficiency in state tax structures. Inevitably, the most burdened states defaulted on their debts and eventually several states repudiated portions of their debts.

Mississippi and Florida defaulted first in 1841, followed shortly by Arkansas and Indiana. Illinois, Michigan, Maryland, Pennsylvania, and Louisiana defaulted in 1842, to bring the total of defaulting states to nine. Several other states narrowly averted the same fate. The collapse in Pennsylvania was the most telling disaster inasmuch as the Keystone state had the largest debt and a long-held reputation for sound financing. Most of Pennsylvania's debt was held in Europe, and foreign investors were bitter in their denunciation of the overextended states.[7] State difficulties led to a movement, foreign as well as domestically inspired, for federal assumption of state debts. The plan was defeated in 1843.[8]

The financial distress of the early 1840's, coupled with a seemingly hopeless burden of debts, resulted in a growing movement in the defaulting states for outright repudiation. Mississippi allowed many of their outstanding bonds to continue in default and refused to redeem the bonds even after a successful bondholders' suit. Repudiation was made final in 1875 by adoption of a constitutional amendment forbidding payment of the questionable bonds. Florida, Arkansas, and Michigan also repudiated portions of their debts on various technical grounds. Total debts repudiated by the four states were as follows:[9]

Arkansas	$ 500,000	Michigan	$2,270,000
Florida	4,000,000	Mississippi	7,000,000

With some adjustments, the remaining five states with bonds in default managed to extricate themselves from their predicament without being charged with repudiation. Nonetheless, bondholders incurred substantial losses because of their failure to collect all back interest and because of rate adjustments made when the states refunded the bonds in default.[10]

The Movement for Constitutional Limitations on State Debt

Taxpayer unrest with the financial plight of the borrowing states resulted in a growing sentiment for permanent restrictions on the debt-incurring power of state legislatures. Rhode Island, although free of debt at the time, led the movement in 1842 by adopting a constitutional amendment (effective in 1843) which read:

The general assembly shall have no power, hereafter, without the express consent of the people, to incur state debts to an amount exceeding fifty thousand dollars, except in time of war, or in case of insurrection or invasion; nor shall they in any case, without such consent, pledge the faith of the state for the payment of the obligations of others.[11]

Although Rhode Island went first, it was for New Jersey, also free of debt, to provide a pattern for debt limitations which has been widely imitated in other states. The New Jersey amendment of 1844 read:

The legislature shall not, in any manner, create any debt or debts, liability or liabilities, of the state, which shall singly or in the aggregate with any previous debts or liabilities at any time exceed one hundred thousand dollars, except for purposes of war, or to repel invasion, or to suppress insurrection, unless the same shall be authorized by a law for some single object or work, to be distinctly specified therein; which law shall provide the ways and means, exclusive of loans, to pay the interest of such debt or the liability as it falls due, and also to pay and discharge its principal of such debt or liability within thirty-five years from the time of the contraction thereof, and shall be irrepealable until such debt or liability, and the interest thereon, are fully paid and discharged; and no such law shall take effect until it shall, at a general election, have been submitted to the people, and have received the sanction of a majority of the votes cast for and against it at such election; and all money to be raised by the authority of such law shall be applied only to the specific object stated therein, and to the payment of the debt thereby created. This section shall not be construed to refer to any money that has been or may be deposited with this State by the government of the United States.[12]

Prior to the Civil War, nineteen states adopted constitutional amendments limiting the amount and purpose of state debt. Several Southern states adopted such amendments during the reconstruction period, and all states subsequently entering the Union have included some restrictive provision in their constitutions. The most recent amendments of significance were adopted by Arkansas in 1934 and North Carolina in 1936 following financial difficulties during the great depression. Both Alaska and Hawaii entered the Union with constitutional debt restrictions, although Hawaii's provision gives its legislature considerable freedom in borrowing matters.[13] Only seven states have never restricted the debt-incurring power of the state legislature, and of those seven, two require special legislative majorities. Table 3 shows states having significant debt limitations and the year of first adoption of those limitations.

Characteristics of Debt Limitations

The types of constitutional debt limitations adopted by states fall into two general categories. In one group, states may borrow for specific projects if given the consent of the people, i.e., a referendum provision. The other group of states are absolutely prohibited from borrowing for most purposes. In the latter group of states, borrowing can take place only if specifically authorized by a constitutional amendment. Within these categories a variety of conditions and exceptions exist:

1. Some small amount, usually a fixed sum, but occasionally a percentage of assessed valuation or debt reduction in a previous year, is exempt from the absolute or referendum restriction. The

TABLE 3

States having significant debt limitations and the year of their adoption

State	Year	State	Year
Ala.	1867	Neb.	1866
Alaska	1958	Nev.	1864
Ariz.	1867	N.J.	1844
Ark.	1934	N.M.	1911
Calif.	1849	N.Y.	1846
Colo.	1876	N.C.	1936
Fla.	1885	N.D.	1889
Ga.	1877	Ohio	1851
Hawaii	1959	Okla.	1907
Idaho	1889	Ore.	1857
Ill.	1848	Pa.	1857
Ind.	1851	R.I.	1842
Iowa	1846	S.C.	1868
Kan.	1855	S.D.	1889
Ky.	1850	Tex.	1845
La.	1845	Utah	1895
Me.	1848	Va.	1870
Md.	1851	Wash.	1889
Mich.	1843	W.Va.	1872
Minn.	1857	Wis.	1848
Mo.	1875	Wyo.	1889
Mont.	1889		

Note: This information was extracted from the constitutions of the various states.

purposes of this exemption may be to cover casual deficits or extraordinary expenses, or in some cases the exemption may be for any purpose. The exempt amounts range from $50,000 to $2,000,000, or to 1½ per cent of assessed valuation. Whereas this amount may have been significant at the time the amendments were adopted when state revenues and expenditures were relatively small, the significance of these exemptions is today nil. The exception to this rule is Hawaii where the legislature is free to borrow up to $60,000,000 for any purpose, and over that amount with a two-thirds vote of its legislators; total state debt cannot exceed 15 per cent of assessed valuation, however. These liberal provisions can undoubtedly be attributed to Hawaii's recent statehood.

2. Where borrowing by referendum is permitted, commonly a specific provision must be incorporated in the borrowing act which would provide revenue for the payment of principal and interest. Some states are required to levy a specific tax—which is irrepealable until the debt is retired—for service of the debt. In other states improvement revenue or special funds may be the stipulated source for debt service.

3. The term of a specific debt issue is commonly limited to a maximum number of years. This restriction also applies to Maryland where the legislature is otherwise free to borrow.

4. Indirect pledging of a state's credit for the benefit of local governments or private individuals is generally prohibited.

5. Borrowing for certain purposes may be exempt from the debt restrictions; these exemptions include defense of the state,

TABLE 4

Provisions of state constitutions governing legislative borrowing power

State	No limitation on borrowing power	Legislative borrowing power limited to specified monetary maximums		May not borrow without popular referendum	Exceptions to limits on borrowing power: may borrow		
		For casual deficits or extraordinary expenses only	For any purpose or for other special purposes		For refunding purposes	For defending state	For other special purposes
Ala.		$ 300,000			X	X^a	
Alaska				X	X	X	
Ariz.		350,000				X	
Ark.				X	X		
Calif.			$ 300,000	X^b		X	
Colo.		100,000	50,000^c				
Conn.	X						
Del.	X^d	—^{e}			X	X	
Fla.					X	X	
Ga.		500,000	3,500,000^f		X	X	
Hawaii			60,000,000		X	X	
Idaho			2,000,000	X^b		X	
Ill.		250,000		X^b		X	
Ind.		—^{e}				X	
Iowa		250,000		X^b		X	
Kan.			1,000,000	X^b		X	
Ky.		500,000		X^b	X	X	
La.		2,000,000			X	X	
Me.			2,000,000	X		X	
Md.	X^g	50,000				X	
Mass.	X^h					X	—^{i}
Mich.		250,000				X	
Minn.		250,000^b	250,000^j			X	—^{k}
Miss.	X						
Mo.		1,000,000^l		X^b	X		
Mont.			100,000^b	X^b		X	
Neb.		100,000				X	
Nev.			—^{m,b}			X	
N.H.	X						
N.J.			—^{n}	X^b		X	—^{o}
N.M.		200,000		X^{b,m}	X	X	
N.Y.				X^b	X	X	—^{p}
N.C.		—^{e}	—^{q}	X	X	X	—^{i}
N.D.			2,000,000^b		X	X	—^{r}
Ohio		750,000			X	X	
Okla.		500,000		X^b		X	
Ore.			50,000			X	—^{s}
Pa.		1,000,000			X	X	
R.I.			50,000	X, X^b	X	X	—^{i}
S.C.		—^{e}			X	X	
S.D.		100,000^b	—^{t}		X	X	—^{u}
Tenn.	X						
Tex.		200,000			X	X	
Utah		—^{m,b}				X	
Vt.	X						
Va.				X^m	X	X	
Wash.		400,000		X^b		X	
W.Va.		—^{e}			X	X	
Wis.		100,000^b				X	
Wyo.			—^{v}	X^m		X	

(Footnotes on page 12)

suppression of insurrection, refunding, and a variety of other purposes. In another unique provision Hawaii specifically exempts projects which are financed by revenue bonds.

In Delaware and Massachusetts the legislature is free to borrow any amount for any purpose, but special majorities of three fourths and two thirds of the legislators, respectively, are required. Five states, New Hampshire, Vermont, Connecticut, Mississippi, and Tennessee, are not constitutionally limited in matters of borrowing. Table 4 presents a summary of constitutional debt provisions as they exist in the states today. Excerpts from state constitutions showing precise provisions of all the states are incorporated in Appendix A.

The intention of the people in adopting the debt limitations previously described seems quite clear. These limitations were intended either to prohibit state borrowing for public improvements or to require public approval of this type of borrowing. Nonetheless, recent developments in the area of state finance have almost completely undermined the restrictive ability of constitutional debt limitations. State borrowing for roads, bridges, public buildings, and harbor improvements—certainly these are works of internal improvement—occurs regularly, restrictions not to the contrary. The next chapter will describe this erosion of the force of constitutional debt restrictions.

---

[a] By two-thirds vote of the legislature.
[b] Provision must be made for payment of interest and/or principal at time of borrowing.
[c] May borrow up to $50,000 for public buildings unless greater amount, not exceeding three mills on the taxable valuation, is approved by popular referendum.
[d] No limits other than a requirement of three-fourths vote in each house.
[e] May borrow for this purpose by no maximum specified.
[f] To pay public school teachers—short-term loans payable out of current funds.
[g] No limits except that provision must be made for payment of interest and principal in fifteen years and referendum requirement for veterans' bonus.
[h] No limits other than two-thirds vote of each house.
[i] Tax or revenue anticipation loans.
[j] For institutional buildings.
[k] Also for rural credits, to prevent forest fires, and for aviation facilities.
[l] For any one year.
[m] Limitation in terms of percentage of assessed valuation of property.
[n] Limitation in terms of percentage of total annual appropriations.
[o] Also for disasters.
[p] Also for forest fires and tax anticipation loans.
[q] Limited to two-thirds amount debt reduced in previous biennium.
[r] Also funds to lend on real estate and $10 million for state enterprise.
[s] Also for specified purposes in terms of percentage of assessed valuation of property.
[t] For internal improvements and rural credit in terms of percentage of assessed valuation of property and by two-thirds vote.
[u] Also to provide funds for coal, cement, and electric enterprises.
[v] Limited to amount of tax revenue for current year.

Source: The Council of State Governments, *Public Authorities in the States* (Chicago: by the Council of State Government, 1953).

Note: Debt provisions in Hawaii and Alaska, taken from their constitutions, were added to this table. For Alaska and Hawaii under exceptions to limits on borrowing power: may borrow, for other special purposes, they may borrow exceptionally for disaster; for Hawaii, for debts over $60,000,000, a two-thirds vote of the legislators is required, but total debt may not exceed 15 per cent of assessed valuation of real property.

2

The Impact of Nonguaranteed

Borrowing on State Debt

STATE AND local debt superficially is subject of severe restrictions. . . . Like too many severe restrictions in America, what is forbidden by one method occurs by another method."[1] This statement well typifies the change in state borrowing procedures since 1900. In 1900 state debt amounted to less than three dollars per capita, and almost all of the debt was guaranteed by the full faith and credit of the borrowing states in accordance with their constitutions. By 1959 long-term state debt was $93.55 per capita, of which $46.78 was nonguaranteed debt largely incurred for purposes expressly prohibited by constitutional provisions. The following sections briefly describe the origin and development of nonguaranteed borrowing methods which have permitted states to borrow outside constitutional restrictions, noting their impact on the composition of state debts.

Nonguaranteed Borrowing Methods

States have developed nonguaranteed borrowing methods by a process of trial and error. When constitutional restrictions stood in the way of borrowing for public purposes, state legislatures improvised methods of borrowing which were, hopefully, beyond constitutional bans. When courts, in the face of taxpayer suits, ruled debt proposals to be unconstitutional, state legislatures altered their proposals until they achieved the sanction of the courts. As a consequence, any history of this phenomenon is a history of the development of judicial interpretation of constitutional debt provisions. This judicial development is well documented in

13

other books and articles;[2] the emphasis in this chapter will be on the practical aspects of this history. For the legally minded, a comprehensive but by no means exhaustive list of the rules of law involved and the cases that established the precedents has been incorporated in Appendix B.

Nonguaranteed borrowing methods can be classified into four broad categories: (1) revenue bonds of state agencies (the special-fund doctrine); (2) public corporations, authorities, and commissions; (3) lease-purchase agreements; and (4) delegation of state functions to political subdivisions. Short-term notes and warrants have been used to avoid debt restrictions, but the importance of this method is today almost negligible.

Revenue bonds and the special-fund doctrine. Specifically, revenue bonds may be defined as "bonds of political units that are payable as to principal and interest exclusively from the earnings, or (in the case of a sale of the property) from other non-contributed assets, of a specified revenue-producing enterprise, for the acquisition, construction, improvement, or operation of which enterprise the bonds were issued."[3] In recent years the term revenue bond has been commonly expanded to include bonds which are serviced out of public funds, the sources of which are rental revenues from other political agencies or units, or special taxes. Occasionally the latter type of bonds are termed quasi-revenue or limited-obligation bonds. For purposes of this study, the term revenue bond will encompass the broad definition and include all bonds of political units not payable out of general funds or otherwise guaranteed by the taxing power of a political unit.

The special-fund doctrine generally holds that debts which are not serviced out of general funds, and are not guaranteed by the full faith and credit of the issuing political unit, are not debts in the meaning of constitutional restrictions. Thus, under this doctrine, revenue bonds are not debt within the meaning of state constitutions. The doctrine as applied takes as many forms as there are states, for the definitions as to what constitutes a pledge of a state's credit or a general fund are within the purview of the courts in the individual states. In several states, for instance, bonds serviced out of and secured by gasoline-tax revenues are not debt for constitutional purposes, while in other states such debt falls under constitutional provisions. The various rules involved are further elaborated in Appendix B.[4]

Colorado took the first step in the establishment of the special-fund doctrine in 1889 by issuing interest bearing certificates to pay for the construction of canals and for the reclamation of state lands. The certificates were payable out of canal revenues and land sales. The Colorado Supreme Court licensed the operation by ruling that the certificates were not state debt because there was no claim on the general fund.[5] (Previously, in 1852, New York had tried to finance canal construction by borrowing $9,000,000 without a referendum as required by the state constitution. The bonds were to be serviced out of surplus canal revenues. In a case unusual in the sense that many of today's arguments pro and con were analyzed, the borrowing was ruled unconstitutional.[6])

After Colorado, many states, not without temporary reversals, adopted and developed versions of the special-fund doctrine. In 1897 the courts permitted Montana to borrow $450,000 for building construction, the debt to be serviced out of land-grant revenues. Minnesota in 1909 was permitted to build a prison with borrowed funds of $2,250,000 to be serviced out of a special tax. The special-fund doctrine has been taken to its furthest reaches in South Carolina. In 1929 the South Carolina legislature authorized the governor to issue bonds payable from revenues of the gasoline tax, and further to pledge the full faith and credit of the state. In its decision the South Carolina Supreme Court ruled that, the bonds being serviced out of an existing tax, the taxpayers could not be harmed; and, further, that pledging the credit of the state only implied that another tax might be used (the property tax was specified) in the event the gasoline tax failed to provide adequate revenues; and hence the bonds were not public debt. In addition, it stated that "This pledge of the faith, credit and taxing power of the state is merely a pledge of Honor, because the State cannot be sued for an enforcement thereof without its consent."[7] Thus, South Carolina may borrow freely, pledging the credit of the state without submitting the borrowing act to a referendum, as required by its constitution.

While other states have not gone to this extreme, all states with constitutional debt limitations have adopted some more or less rigorous form of the special-fund doctrine.[8] In some states, courts seem to require that a special agency or public corporation act as the issuing agency; this development will be discussed in the following section. The crux of the matter is that, with proper manipulation of borrowing technique to fit the rules of law of a particular state, a state may use revenue bonds to finance public improvements that were seemingly prohibited when constitutional debt limitations were adopted.

Public corporations, authorities, and commissions. In states where the special-fund doctrine in its more strict sense did not meet the courts' approval, the states adopted a "new conception" and "more subtle subterfuge"[9] in the public authority. Basically, the public authority is a corporate body created to serve a public purpose and empowered to issue revenue bonds to be serviced and secured by the income of that body. For the most part, courts have ruled that authority debt is not public debt.

While other logical reasons have been cited for the establishment of public authorities,[10] certainly their exemption from constitutional debt provisions is a dominant reason. Loosely defined, the special-fund doctrine may be said to encompass the use of public authorities as a method of circumventing debt limitations; but for purposes of the discussion in this chapter revenue bonds of public authorities will be distinguished from revenue bonds of regular state agencies.

While the authority plan may be traced as far back as 1899 to the Kennebec Water District in Maine,[11] the modern movement began in 1921 with the creation of the Port of New York Authority by New York and New Jersey.[12] Actually, the Port of New York Authority was created not for constitutional circumvention, but to solve the political and geographical problems created by the location of the port between New York and New Jersey; however, the format used has served as a basis for other public corporations created for a more "devious" purpose. Other states which shortly followed the lead were New Jersey with the South Jersey Port Commission and Alabama with its State Bridge Corporation in 1926, California with its Toll Bridge Authority in 1929, and Georgia and New York in 1931 with the Augusta Canal

Commission and the Power Authority of the State of New York, respectively.

The great depression of the 1930's served to strengthen the authority movement. This was abetted by no less than the federal government. The Reconstruction Finance Corporation was created in 1931 and empowered to lend $1.5 million to public bodies for the construction and operation of self-liquidating projects. The program was handicapped by the lack of legislation in many states authorizing the creation of public corporations and the issuance of revenue bonds. President Roosevelt sent letters to state governors in 1934 suggesting a legislative program to correct this need. He recommended legislation authorizing existing state agencies to issue revenue bonds and enabling legislation for the creation of public corporations. Acceptance of the proposal was widespread, and between 1933 and 1936 nineteen states passed legislation creating public authorities empowered to issue revenue bonds.

The authority movement has achieved its greatest momentum since World War II. Its use in port and power development and toll bridges has been expanded. Since 1945 authorities have been created to construct and operate toll roads, school buildings, hospitals, parks, and state office buildings, among other public improvements. Whereas the public authority as originally designed received its income from user charges on the public, a significant portion of authority revenues now comes from rental of facilities to state and local governments. (This feature will be further discussed in the next section.) Currently, public authorities with revenue bond powers are operating in thirty-one states with a total revenue debt of $5,671 million outstanding in 1958.

The organization and autonomy of public authorities vary from state to state. In many instances, authorities do not have corporate status,[13] but they do have corporate attributes such as the right to sue and be sued and liability for torts. Members of the governing board may be appointive, ex officio, or elective, or a combination of the first two. Although there is some variation, most public authorities have a high degree of autonomy in personnel, accounting procedures, budgeting, and most other matters. In numerous instances not even a periodic report is required by the state government.[14] In its 1953 study of public authorities, the Council of State Governments has presented a comprehensive study of forty-two authorities in twenty states noting the prevalence of the above and many more of the powers and characteristics of public authorities.[15]

To what extent growth of the public authority can be attributed to its borrowing power as opposed to other reasons for its existence cannot be determined. I suspect that its ability to borrow outside state constitutions is its *raison d'être*. In any event, this power does exist and is widely used in states with constitutional limitations on state debt.

Lease-purchase agreements. Lease-purchase agreements, or installment buying, are not new in the United States, although they pose a relatively new innovation in state finance. The question of a state's ability to sign a lease in the face of debt limitations arose as far back as 1860 in California when the court ruled that an ordinary lease is not a debt because no payment is required until services are received.[16] The substance of this rather clear decision has been carried forward to make possible agreements by which a state may lease facilities built with funds borrowed by private corporations or other governmental units, at rentals sufficient to operate the facilities and amortize the debt. In these cases title to the facility usually reverts to the state government after the amortization period. The legal intricacies involved are significant, and it is never quite clear when a debt is a debt. Occasionally, a simple change in the wording of the lease makes constitutional a project which a few *ands, ifs,* and *buts* ago was unconstitutional.[17]

The leasing arrangement is used extensively in state finance for a variety of purposes. In Pennsylvania the General State Authority constructs school buildings and leases them to school districts that are barred from borrowing because of local debt limitations. The General State Authority itself is a public corporation which issues revenue bonds[18] because of Pennsylvania's absolute debt limit. Arkansas and Wisconsin, among other states, have constructed office buildings by use of the lease-purchase technique. Florida uses a complicated system of leasing between the state and local units of government to finance highway construction.[19] In other states lease-purchase agreements have been variously used to finance hospitals, parks, athletic fields, and armories.

The lease-purchase technique is commonly used in conjunction with the public corporation. The primary purpose of combining the two is to afford a method by which title to the property concerned may pass to the state government after the debt has been amortized. In substance the technique might work as follows: the state legislature creates a public, nonprofit corporation for the special purpose of constructing a state building. Officials of the corporation might be the governor, state treasurer, head of the department using the building, and other officials appointed by the governor to administer the operation. The state sells or leases a building site to the corporation which issues revenue bonds for construction of a building on that site. The corporation then leases the building and site back to the state at a rental sufficient to maintain the building and corporation and to amortize the revenue debt incurred, the rental revenue acting as security for the revenue bonds. The lease stipulates that title to the building revert to the state government after the debt is amortized. Normally the public corporation then becomes inactive until another project comes along.[20]

The administrative and contractual intricacies vary, because the legal criteria for determining the constitutionality of such borrowing differ from state to state. The lease-purchase method of financing public buildings has become so refined in most debt-limit states that borrowing for construction of public buildings for any purpose may be readily accomplished. All that is required is that the administrative organization and contractual relationships be molded into the pattern previously passed as constitutional by the state courts.

Delegation of state functions to political subdivisions. When a state is faced with a debt limit, and local units have more freedom to borrow, the state can finance particular government functions by delegating those functions to local units. This may be done explicitly because of the debt-limit problem; but, more commonly, the debt problem is but one of the factors involved. Some functions are clearly proper (within our political framework) for the state government to provide. Others are clearly within the province of local units. There exist, however, a host of functions that may well be performed by either the state or its political subdivisions. When the problem is resolved, one of the factors that undoubtedly enters is the borrowing capacity of the political units involved. For example, in Wisconsin counties have the responsibility for the construction and maintenance of the highway system. In other states the state government largely performs the same function. Many factors are involved in the division of such functions, and it is impossible to assess the relative importance of debt limitations.

In some cases the use of this technique is clearly identifiable as an evasion of debt limitations. States have used forms of reimbursement obligations for years in the financing of state highways. Highways were originally a local function, but the development of the truck and automobile necessitated the construction of a comprehensive interstate and intrastate system of roads. Planning of this nature could not be left to local units of government, and as a result the federal and state highway systems emerged. When states absorbed county highways into the state systems, counties clamored for state assumption of the debts incurred in their construction. In many instances debt limits made outright refunding and assumption impossible, but states established various methods by which they could service the counties' debts without running afoul of state constitutions. Although the reimbursement technique varies widely among the states, in substance it is operated by the state government returning sufficient funds to the counties to pay the principal and/or interest on debt incurred for construction of highways which are part of the state system.[21]

Reimbursement obligations have decreased in importance, probably because of the refinement of other methods of borrowing outside constitutional limitations. In 1945 reimbursement obligations outstanding totaled $136 million, but by 1957 the amount had fallen to $46 million.

Growth of State Debt

The impact of these developments on the growth and structure of state debt can be seen from data on the growth of total long-term debt and nonguaranteed long-term debt[22] as presented in

TABLE 5

State long-term debt, full faith and credit and nonguaranteed, for selected years, 1930–1958

Year	Long-term debt (millions)			Non-guaranteed debt as a percentage of total debt	Total debt as a percentage of personal income
	Total	Full faith and credit	Non-guaranteed		
1930	$ 2,444	$ —	$ —	—	3.36
1937	3,023	2,983	40	1.3	4.14
1940	3,042	2,854	188	6.2	4.08
1945	2,522	2,156	366	14.5	1.62
1948	3,484	2,983	368	10.6	1.69
1950	5,150	4,467	883	17.9	2.30
1951	5,974	4,688	1,286	21.6	2.38
1952	6,640	4,926	1,714	25.8	2.49
1953	7,504	5,158	2,347	31.3	2.67
1954	9,317	5,770	3,547	38.1	3.29
1955	10,950	5,929	5,022	45.9	3.63
1956	12,643	6,213	6,430	50.9	4.00
1957	13,522	6,490	7,032	52.0	4.06
1958	15,065	7,349	7,716	51.1	4.40

Source: Bureau of the Census, *Compendium of State Government Finances*, 1930–1959

Table 5. Whereas the amount of nonguaranteed debt in 1930 was negligible, and only $366 million or 15 per cent of total long-term debt in 1945, it had grown to $7,716 million and 51 per cent of total long-term state debt by 1958. Between 1945 and 1958, full-faith and credit debt only increased 240 per cent, but non-guaranteed debt went up 2000 per cent. In the face of these figures there seems little doubt that the emergence of revenue bonds and public authorities has played an important role in state debt finance since 1930.

Despite the widespread use of nonguaranteed borrowing, the burden of state debt has not increased very much, contrary to common conception. In recent years considerable alarm has been shown over the rapid rise in state debt. Table 5 shows that state debt increased six times between 1945 and 1958. This fact has been brought out on numerous occasions to dramatize the need for new sources of state revenue and for federal aid to states for education and redevelopment, among other purposes. A closer look at Table 5 reveals that state debt as a percentage of personal income, a far better measure of debt burden than absolute debt, is very little higher in 1958 than in 1940. This certainly does not

TABLE 6

State revenue debt, exclusive of public authority debt, outstanding at
end of fiscal year 1958, by purpose of issue (thousands of dollars)

State	Debt outstanding				
	Bridges and highways	Higher education	State institutions	Miscel-laneous	Total
Ala.	$ —	$ 9,238	$ —	$ —	$ 9,238
Ariz.	13,212	27	—	—	13,239
Ark.	—	19,382	1,600	10	20,992
Colo.	27,804	24,307	847	—	52,958
Conn.	285,000	—	—	—	285,000
Del.	22,190	—	—	14,807	36,997
Fla.	—	18,406	176	36	18,618
Ga.	—	1,740	—	—	1,740
Idaho	—	4,258	—	—	4,258
Ill.	—	40,827	—	—	40,827
Ind.	—	74,525	276	—	74,801
Iowa	—	12,004	—	—	12,004
Kan.	—	11,069	—	—	11,069
Ky.	47,246	15,895	—	—	63,141
La.	—	26,821	4,313	3,536	34,670
Me.	32,251	1,801	—	—	34,052
Md.	165,848	5,464	—	—	171,312
Mich.	211,689	114,893	—	—	326,582
Minn.	—	12,228	—	—	12,228
Miss.	84,448	377	—	—	84,825
Mo.	—	11,906	—	—	11,906
Mont.	3,000	15,584	169	19,217	37,970
Neb.	9,409	—	—	280	9,689
N.H.	—	137	—	—	137
N.J.	—	5,355	—	—	5,355
N.M.	—	20,877	1,242	2,777	24,896
N.C.	—	4,709	—	—	4,709
N.D.	—	4,701	—	—	4,701
Ohio	315,490	38,859	—	—	354,349
Okla.	—	30,601	—	—	30,601
Ore.	—	93	—	—	93
Pa.	—	22,600	—	—	22,600
R.I.	—	1,237	—	—	1,237
S.C.	—	12,041	334	—	12,375
S.D.	—	4,734	—	—	4,734
Tenn.	—	4,118	—	—	4,118
Tex.	—	68,611	—	—	68,611
Utah	—	5,991	—	—	5,991
Va.	95,000	7,931	—	402	103,333
Wash.	76,560	18,772	—	172,151	267,483
W.Va.	1,395	2,971	75	—	4,441
Wyo.	—	3,248	—	216	3,464
Total	$1,390,542	$678,338	$9,032	$213,432	$2,291,344

Note: This table was constructed from unpublished data made available by the Bureau of the Census.

indicate that states have been overburdening themselves with debt compared to the past. It is true that with 1945 as a base, state debt has significantly increased as a percentage of personal income; but 1945 was an unusual year. It was the end of a war period during which states were paying off debt. If we neglect the effects of the 1941–1945 period, Table 5 shows that state debt burden has increased very little since 1930. The main effect of public authorities and the special-fund doctrine has apparently been to change the character of state debt and not to increase the burden appreciably.

The Structure of Nonguaranteed Debt in 1958

From almost negligible proportions thirty years ago, state revenue bonds outstanding had grown to $2,291 million by 1958. Table 6 shows the amount and purpose of revenue bonds, exclusive of the bonds of public authorities, outstanding in the various states at the end of the fiscal year 1958. Thirty-nine states have issued revenue bonds for state colleges aggregating $678 million. Even more important in aggregate amount is the $1,390 million outstanding for highways and bridges in fifteen states. Debt issued for these two purposes constitutes 90 per cent of the total revenue debt (exclusive of the debts of public authorities)

TABLE 7

Reimbursement obligations outstanding at end of fiscal years 1945, 1950, 1957
(thousands of dollars)

State	1945	1950	1957
Ala.	$ —	$ —	$ 2,923
Conn.	6,266	—	—
Del.	3,870	2,370	1,135
Fla.	3,954	3,841	28,820
Iowa	34,458	—	—
Kan.	12,240	6,840	96
La.	—	53	—
Mo.	—	92	91
Ore.	23	—	—
S.C.	6,274	1,966	1,346
Tenn.	6,932	6	—
Tex.	60,188	30,959	7,723
Wash.	146	83	—
Wis.	2,399	3,553	4,019
Total	$136,750	$49,763	$46,153

Source: Bureau of Public Roads, *Highway Statistics*, 1946, 1951, and 1958.

outstanding in 1958. In the meantime, reimbursement obligations outstanding declined, as shown in Table 7.

Even more spectacular has been the rapid growth of state authorities. From none in 1926, and less than $135 million in 1940, the aggregate debt of state authorities had grown to $5,671 million by 1958.[23] Table 8 shows the outstanding revenue debts of state authorities by purpose of the debt at the end of the fiscal year 1958. The use of the authority device for toll roads and bridges outweighs all other uses combined.[24] Ranking next are water and power authorities, largely because of New York's huge power authority with its revenue debt of over $349 million in 1958, and the public power districts in Nebraska. These two authority types along with port authorities may generally be differentiated from the other categories of authorities listed in Table 8, because they operate as well as finance public projects. Nontoll

TABLE 8

Revenue debt of state authorities[a] outstanding at end of
fiscal year 1958, by purpose of issue
(thousands of dollars)

State	Toll roads and bridges	Nontoll highway	Education	Public power and water	Ports	State office buildings	Miscellaneous	Total
Ala.	$ —	$ 53,100	$ —	$ —	$10,725	$ 6,945	$ 1,050	$ 71,820
Ark.	—	—	—	—	—	1,600	—	1,600
Calif.	108,000	4,934	—	—	5,442	—	—	118,376
Colo.	—	—	—	—	—	1,798	—	1,798
Fla.	162,481	29,830	—	—	—	2,340	—	194,651
Ga.	5,682	102,578	154,035	—	5,200	10,356	17,502	295,353
Ill.	441,279	—	—	—	—	—	6,413	447,692
Ind.	280,000	—	—	—	—	30,000	600	310,600
Kan.	175,468	—	—	—	—	7,500	2,575	185,543
Ky.	—	—	—	—	—	5,379	7,615	12,994
La.	65,000	—	—	—	—	—	4,313	69,313
Me.	78,600	—	4,071	—	100	—	—	82,771
Md.	—	170,291	—	—	—	—	—	170,291
Mass.	262,539	—	7,674	—	—	—	6,562	276,775
Mich.	99,800	—	—	—	—	—	—	99,800
Miss.	—	—	—	—	—	—	300	300
Neb.	—	—	—	262,700	—	—	—	262,700
N.H.	—	—	—	904	—	—	—	904
N.J.	494,239	—	—	—	—	—	—	494,239
N.Y.	407,972	—	20,555	349,050	—	—	6,322	783,899
Ohio	326,000	—	—	—	—	—	—	326,000
Okla.	104,696	—	—	21,477	—	—	6,584	132,757
Pa.	442,916	78,431	126,194	—	—	—	252,217	899,758
R.I.	2,468	—	—	—	—	—	216	2,684
S.C.	1,500	—	—	49,351	—	—	446	51,297
Tex.	58,500	—	—	51,261	—	—	—	109,761
Va.	75,150	—	—	—	—	—	—	75,150
Wash.	37,070	—	—	—	—	—	—	37,070
W.Va.	133,000	—	—	—	—	1,395	4,420	138,815
Wis.	—	—	10,829	—	—	4,474	—	15,303
Wyo.	—	—	—	—	—	992	—	992
Total	$3,762,360	$439,164	$323,358	$734,743	$21,467	$72,779	$317,135	$5,671,006

[a] Does not include the debts of interstate authorities.
Note: This table was constructed from unpublished data made available by the Bureau of the Census and from my own survey of state authorities.

highway and bridge authorities, education building authorities, and office building authorities normally function only for finance purposes, the operation of the projects being left to regular state agencies. The former category may also be distinguished because the authorities generally rely on public user charges for revenues, while the latter category of authorities depends upon state appropriations, rentals, and special taxes.

Is Nonguaranteed Debt State Debt?

It is quite clear that the debts of state authorities and state revenue bonds are state debts in the sense that the projects and methods of financing were conceived and authorized by state legislatures. It also seems clear that state authorities and state agencies issuing revenue bonds are financial arms or instrumentalities of the states. The Internal Revenue Service has accepted this latter point as grounds for exempting the income from revenue bonds from federal income taxes.[25] On the other hand, courts have generally held that states are not liable for revenue bonds or for the bonds of public authorities in the sense that the bondholders have no ultimate claim against state property or general tax funds, and hence that these bonds do not constitute state debts. In the face of these contradictions, can a state be labeled hypocritical when it stamps its envelopes "Indiana, where we live within our income," when that state has a per capita nonguaranteed debt nearly as large as the average per capita debt, guaranteed and nonguaranteed, for all states?

One issue at hand is the question of a state's moral and political responsibility for the debts of its instrumentalities. For instance, is the State of Wisconsin morally responsible for making good on the dormitory bonds of its University Building Corporation should dormitory revenues prove inadequate to service the bonds? Revenue bonds generally carry the name of the issuing state in bold letters, and occasionally have the state seal. Under these circumstances, could state legislators sit back and boldly disclaim any responsibility?

Presumably, state projects are undertaken because they are expected to provide important public services. Failure of a project to generate sufficient revenues for debt service, while perhaps implying error in beginning the project, does not mean that it is politically or economically wise to discontinue the service of the project. Ratchford cites an example in which a financial downturn results in decreased appropriations to state agencies. In order to meet its fixed interest charges on revenue bonds, an agency may have to impair other services radically.[26] It seems rather unlikely that a state would reduce its rentals on office buildings constructed by a state corporation, thereby throwing the bonds into default, and perhaps foreclose use of the building to the state. In one study, the author states:

> The question here involves the moral responsibility of the State towards the bondholders. It is inconceivable that private bondholders would be allowed to foreclose on the Turnpike if revenues should ever prove to be insufficient to cover debt charges. The public nature of the Turnpike, plus the unfavorable effect on the State's credit standing, would seem to be grounds for preventing such foreclosure. In the dismal event that bankruptcy should ever face the Authority, it seems probable that the State would assume the responsibility for the unpaid bonds. Because of this it is reasonable that the Turnpike bonds should be recognized as contingent liabilities of the State.[27]

Perhaps the most important question is: would various states, *in fact,* make good on defaulted revenue bonds? Alabama made good on the defaulted bonds of the Alabama State Bridge Corporation in 1936. When its state capitol bonds which were secured by land-grant revenues were forced into default in 1939, Montana payed off the revenue bondholders by refunding with general obligations. Currently, bonds of the West Virginia Turnpike are in default, but the final result is not yet in. Bondholders apparently have some belief that states would make good. State authorities have used 100 per cent bond financing on most projects at interest rates comparing favorably with private bond financing which has a 50 per cent or more cushion of equity capital. If investors thought differently, surely 100 per cent bond financing would not be available to state authorities. On the other hand, investors do not consider revenue bonds to be as secure as general obligations. If they did there would be no interest rate differential between the two types of bonds.

Because of its extralegal character, one cannot come to a definite conclusion as to a state's intentions regarding its revenue bonds. It seems likely that many states would like to impress investors that state intentions are strong in order to secure more favorable interest rates, but these intentions cannot be put into the bond indentures lest the constitutionality of the project be endangered. Investors can never be as sure of state backing with revenue bonds as they can be with general obligations because they do not receive a state pledge in the contract, and hence they have fewer legal remedies available. If a state fully intends to pay off its revenue obligations regardless of the outcome of the project for which the obligations were issued, and cannot make those intentions perfectly clear because of constitutional restrictions against a pledge of state credit, it gives rise to what might be termed a "risk gap"—a gap between the actual risk that a state might repudiate its revenue bonds as determined by its intentions, and the risk envisioned by the investors in revenue bonds. A risk gap will exist whenever a state fully intends its revenue bonds to be as secure as general obligations but cannot put those intentions into the bond indenture because of constitutional limitations.

Conclusions

The courts' sanction of revenue bonds, public authorities, lease-purchase agreements, and reimbursement obligations as legitimate methods of state borrowing despite constitutional debt prohibitions has radically changed the structure of state debt. These innovations in state finance have enabled states to borrow for almost any purpose regardless of constitutional provisions. It seems reasonable to conclude that constitutional debt restrictions are no longer accomplishing that which they were originally intended to accomplish. It also seems clear that debt restrictions do have an important impact in that they force restricted states to use other than full-faith and credit borrowing. Some claim that this effect acts as a significant deterrent to state borrowing and, while not all that they desire, is better than no deterrent at all. This contention will be analyzed in the next chapter.

The Effectiveness of Constitutional Debt Restrictions

THE ANALYSIS in the preceding chapter clearly indicates that present constitutional debt restrictions do not prevent states from borrowing for public projects. Opponents of constitutional revision would cheerfully concede this observation, while clinging to the notion that present restrictions significantly impede excessive state borrowing. They believe that the difficulty in molding state debt programs into a constitutionally acceptable framework forestalls impetuous excursions into borrowing for state projects. This contention would have been more acceptable thirty years ago, however, when nonguaranteed borrowing devices were still in the development stage. Most restricted states have now cleared the development hurdle and have reached the stage where they can borrow freely by molding borrowing procedures into old patterns.

The ultimate test of effectiveness of debt restrictions would involve a comparison of state borrowing over a certain time period with such restrictions, against state borrowing over the same time period without restrictions. Such a test obviously cannot be made. It is not possible to determine what a particular state's debt position would currently be if constitutional debt provisions had been different in the past. This conundrum does not foreclose the possibility of reaching some conclusions as to the effectiveness of constitutional debt limitations.

A Test of Effectiveness

One method of judging the force of constitutional debt prohibitions is based on a comparison of the debt experience of

states with different debt provisions. On finding that a group of
states without debt restrictions had incurred significantly more
debt than other states with restrictions, one could conclude that
debt restrictions had a measurable effect in limiting the amount
of state debt. Such tests have been run using categories of states
according to similarity of debt provisions. The categories most
commonly selected have been those formulated by the Council of
State Governments in its study of public authorities.[1] They have
categorized states into three groups:

1. *States with no effective debt limitation.* These states can
borrow through legislative action with generally no limits as to
amount or purpose of debt they may incur. States in this category
are:

Connecticut	Massachusetts	Tennessee
Delaware	Mississippi	Vermont
Maryland	New Hampshire	

2. *States with referendum requirements.* This group of states
can generally borrow any amount for any purpose, but only after
each specific debt proposal has been approved by the electorate in
a referendum. Included in this group are:

Arkansas	Maine	Oklahoma
California	Missouri	Rhode Island
Idaho	Montana	South Carolina
Illinois	New Jersey	Virginia
Iowa	New Mexico	Washington
Kansas	New York	Wyoming
Kentucky	North Carolina	

3. *States prohibited from borrowing.* In this group of states,
borrowing generally can take place only after constitutional
amendments exempting particular issues from debt restrictions.[2]
States included are:

Alabama	Michigan	Pennsylvania
Arizona	Minnesota	South Dakota
Colorado	Nebraska	Texas
Florida	Nevada	Utah
Georgia	North Dakota	West Virginia
Indiana	Ohio	Wisconsin
Louisiana	Oregon	

One test using the above categories was run by B. U. Ratchford on debt figures for 1957.[3] Aggregating figures for the three groups of states, he obtained the results shown in Table 9. From his results Ratchford concluded that, while debt limits did not prevent states from borrowing, they did tend to restrict the absolute size of the debt. Table 9 shows that per capita borrowing in the free

TABLE 9

Measures of state debt according to methods of authorizing borrowing
(long-term debt at end of fiscal year 1957)

	States which authorize borrowing by			
	Constitutional amendment Group 3 (20 states)	Referendum Group 2 (20 states)	Legislative action Group 1 (8 states)	Total (48 states)
Total debt (thousands)				
Full faith and credit	$1,482,502	$3,664,345	$1,343,417	$ 6,490,264
Nonguaranteed	3,153,795	2,880,841	997,044	7,031,706
Total	$4,636,297	$6,545,186	$2,340,461	$13,521,970
Per capita debt				
Full faith and credit	$20.22	$46.27	$ 79.13	$38.30
Nonguaranteed	43.02	36.38	58.73	41.49
Total	$63.24	$82.65	$137.86	$79.79
Total debt as a per cent of personal income				
Full faith and credit	1.06	2.30	3.98	1.95
Nonguaranteed	2.25	1.81	2.96	2.11
Total	3.31	4.11	6.94	4.06

Source: Bureau of the Census, *Census of Governments*, 1957, vol. III, No. 5 (hereafter referred to as *1957 Census*).
Note: These figures were calculated from data for the individual states.

Group 1 states was over twice that of the absolutely restricted Group 3 states, and almost 70 per cent greater than that of the referendum Group 2 states. He also noted the apparent contradiction that nonguaranteed borrowing was greater in the Group 1 states than in the other states. While the latter point testifies to the fact that the unrestricted states have found use for nonguaranteed borrowing, it should be pointed out that this result is largely due to *one* nonguaranteed toll road project in Connecticut ($250 million), special tax highway revenue bonds ($70 million) issued years ago by Mississippi, and Maryland's large nonguaranteed debt. Since 1957 Connecticut has completed its toll road by issuing general obligations ($112 million), and Mississippi's recent borrowing ($30 million) has been with general obligations.

In the face of other considerations, however, conclusions based on the results shown in Table 9 are incomplete. One of the states in Group 1, Maryland, has a deceptively forceful debt limitation, and might well be included in Group 3. Maryland's constitution limits state obligations to a maximum term of fifteen years. Inasmuch as a fifteen-year limit forecloses the use of general obligations for projects in which the amortization period is longer, Maryland has turned to the use of revenue bonds and the public authority to escape the limit. In 1957 Maryland's total debt exceeded $520 million, of which $342 million was nonguaranteed. Readjusting to include Maryland in Group 3, the results are

TABLE 10

Measures of state debt for Groups 1 and 3 with Maryland included in Group 3
(long-term debt at the end of fiscal year 1957)

	States which authorize borrowing by	
	Constitutional amendment, Group 3 (including Maryland, 21 states)	Legislative action Group 1 (not including Maryland, 7 states)
Total debt (thousands)		
Full faith and credit	$1,660,399	$1,165,520
Nonguaranteed	3,496,172	654,667
Total	$5,156,571	$1,820,187
Per capita debt		
Full faith and credit	$21.79	$82.77
Nonguaranteed	45.88	46.48
Total	$67.67	$129.25
Total debt as a per cent of personal income		
Full faith and credit	1.13	4.24
Nonguaranteed	2.39	2.38
Total	3.52	6.62

Source: *1957 Census.*
Note: These figures were calculated from data for the individual states.

shown in Table 10. While the basic results are not changed, the differences between the groups of states are narrowed.

Local Debt Considered

Another important consideration is the division of public functions between state and local governments. In line with the analysis of the previous chapter, debt limitations may influence the delegation of functions to political subdivisions of a state. Because of this factor, borrowing for a particular function may show up as state debt in a free state and as local debt in a restricted state. Beyond any conscious delegation of particular functions to avoid state debt limits, there may be inherent differences in the autonomy of the states in each of the groups. In small states such as Delaware, there may be economic and political reasons why particular functions which frequently require borrowing remain with the state government. If this is a large factor in the Group 1 or free states, then state debt in those states would tend to be higher regardless of any constitutional restrictions in other states. Possibly another important factor is the classification employed by the Census Bureau when it compiles state and local debt figures. Often there is a tenuous line between state and local debt, especially when special districts are involved. For instance, the Census Bureau includes the debts of Nebraska's public power districts in local debt rather than in state debt. Because of these factors, local debt must be considered in any quantitative determination of the effectiveness of state debt restrictions. Using the classifications in the previous section, state and local debt figures for 1957 were combined to give the results shown in Table 11.

The relationship between the Group 3 and the Group 1 states minus Maryland is basically unchanged by the inclusion of local debt. Local debt in the Group 3 states was only slightly less than local debt in the Group 1 states minus Maryland. If delegation of state functions to avoid limits or differences in state autonomy were important, they were offset by other factors. Including Maryland in the Group 3 states would raise the per capita state debt to $67.67, per capita local debt to $199.25, and the total per capita debt to $266.92. While the differential between the groups would thereby be narrowed, a significant differential would still exist.

TABLE 11

Measures of state and local debt according to methods of authorizing borrowing
(long-term debt at end of fiscal year 1957)

| | States which authorize borrowing by | | | | |
	Constitutional amendment Group 3 (20 states)	Referendum Group 2 (20 states)	Legislative action Group 1 (8 states)	Legislative action Group 1 (less Maryland, 7 states)	Total (48 states)
State debt (thousands)	$ 4,636,297	$ 6,545,186	$2,340,461	$1,820,187	$13,521,970
Local debt (thousands)	14,258,158	19,353,084	3,673,975	2,759,741	37,285,217
Total debt (thousands)	$18,894,455	$25,898,270	$6,014,436	$4,579,928	$50,807,187
Per capita state debt	$ 63.24	$ 82.65	$137.86	$129.25	$ 79.79
Per capita local debt	194.48	244.37	216.41	195.76	220.01
Total per capita debt	$257.72	$327.02	$354.27	$325.01	$299.80
State debt as a per cent of personal income	3.31	4.11	6.94	6.62	4.06
Local debt as a per cent of personal income	10.17	12.15	10.89	10.04	11.19
Total debt as a per cent of personal income	13.48	16.26	17.83	16.66	15.25

Source: *1957 Census.*
Note: These figures were calculated from data for the individual states.

On the other hand, local debt was significantly higher in the Group 2 states. Indeed, the per capita state and local debt was higher in those states than in the Group 1 states less Maryland. If avoidance of debt limits and differences in state autonomy constitute the main reasons for the greater local debt in the referendum states, then one could conclude that referendum provisions had little or no effect in limiting the total debt burden on state taxpayers.

The Burden of Interest on State and Local Debt

In the previous analyses, one important consideration was omitted: the burden of interest costs on public debts in the various groups of states. Outstanding state and local debts indicate only the face amount of debts that must be repaid at maturity and not the amount of yearly appropriations necessary to service outstanding debts. If the interest charges on state and local debt are higher in Group 2 and Group 3 states, because of constitutional restrictions, then the Group 1 states can carry greater debts than the restricted states without carrying a greater burden. In line with this consideration, the interest charges on state and local debt for the various groups of states in 1957 were determined and the results shown in Table 12.

The results show that the burden of interest charges on state and local debt in the Group 1 states, with or without Maryland, both per capita and as a per cent of personal income, was less than the interest burden in the Group 2 states, despite the fact

TABLE 12

Measures of interest payments on state and local debt according to methods of authorizing borrowing (fiscal year 1957)

	States which authorize borrowing by				
	Constitutional amendment Group 3 (20 states)	Referendum Group 2 (20 states)	Legislative action Group 1 (8 states)	Legislative action Group 1 (less Maryland, 7 states)	Total (48 states)
Interest payments (thousands)					
State	$118,650	$179,307	$ 52,953	$ 41,374	$ 350,910
Local	391,671	534,556	98,073	74,427	1,025,300
Total	$510,321	$713,853	$151,026	$115,801	$1,376,210
Per capita interest payments					
State	$1.62	$2.26	$3.12	$2.94	$2.07
Local	5.34	6.74	5.78	5.29	6.05
Total	$6.96	$9.00	$8.90	$8.23	$8.12
Interest payments as a per cent of personal income					
State	.0846	.1126	.1570	.1505	.1053
Local	.2793	.3357	.2908	.2708	.3077
Total	.3639	.4483	.4478	.4213	.4130

Source: *1957 Census.*
Note: These figures were calculated from data for the individual states.

that outstanding debts were relatively greater in the Group 1 states. Whereas per capita state and local debt was 26 per cent higher in the Group 1 states less Maryland than in the Group 3 states, the per capita interest burden in 1957 was only 18 per cent higher. The same relationship holds with regard to state debt only. While per capita state debt in the Group 1 states minus Maryland was 55 per cent greater than in the Group 2 states and 104 per cent greater than in the Group 3 states, per capita interest payments of the same Group 1 states were only 30 per cent and 78 per cent greater than per capita interest payments of Group 2 and Group 3 states, respectively. No matter how the relationships are presented, the conclusion is similar. When the burden of interest charges on state and local debt is considered, the unrestricted states have done very well indeed.

Conclusions

What could one conclude from the foregoing analyses? The data do not prove that constitutional debt restrictions do not limit state debt. On the other hand, the data do not prove that debt restrictions have limited state debt either. A fair conclusion would seem to be that constitutional provisions have been less effective—if effective at all—in limiting state debt than most people would have supposed. It also seems clear that states currently having unlimited borrowing power have not exhibited a tendency to incur excessive debt. When local debt and the burden of interest charges on debt are taken into account, states with unlimited borrowing power had a smaller debt burden than referendum states in 1957, and not much greater debt burden than absolutely restricted states in 1957.

With complete freedom to borrow, why have state legislatures in unrestricted states limited state borrowing to reasonable levels? Presumably, it must be because the legislators have found it politically and economically prudent to do so. Similarly, why have state legislatures in other states limited their use of revenue bonds in financing state projects? There are few legal limits to the use of revenue bonds. Again, the answer must be found in the political and economic prudence of the legislators. If this is the case, taxpayers ought not to fear the consequences of restoring borrowing power to state legislatures.

Additional Interest Costs
of Nonguaranteed Borrowing

IN GENERAL, revenue bonds tend to carry higher interest costs
than general obligations with comparable covenants. Presumably, this relationship exists because investors normally prefer
the security of an unlimited government tax guarantee to the
specific pledge of special taxes, user charge revenues, or rental
revenues which commonly apply to revenue bonds. Then, too,
some states have prohibited the investment of public funds and
some types of institutional funds in nonguaranteed public obligations. It has been suggested that the latter is the primary reason
for the interest differential; however, strong logic would have to
credit the former reason as being the ultimate determinant. If
investors at large were convinced that nonguaranteed obligations
were the equal of general obligations, individual investors would
be quick to buy revenue bonds as soon as their yield rose substantially above the yield on comparable general obligations, a
move which would tend to negate the price differential. Inasmuch
as this study is concerned primarily with the existence of the
differential and not with investor psychology leading to the differential, this question will not be pursued further.

What evidence is available on the subject tends to confirm the
conclusion that an interest differential exists between revenue
bonds and general obligations.[1] The evidence is rather spotty,
however, and not of general applicability. It is the function of the
following sections to provide more complete evidence and to provide more precise techniques for approximating the added interest
cost of specific revenue financed projects.

Interest Costs on State Debt

One crude method of determining interest differentials arising out of alternative use of guaranteed and nonguaranteed borrowing techniques is to compare debt service charges with outstanding debt in groups of states with varying degrees of reliance on the two borrowing methods. For this comparison two measures are needed: (1) debt service charges as a percentage of the average of the total state debt outstanding at the beginning and end of the year; and (2) the percentage of the total debt in the form of nonguaranteed obligations. This comparison is interesting mainly because it enables a comparison based upon all state debt on the books during any year regardless of when the debt was incurred. The cost of gathering the voluminous data required for a precise analysis of individual state obligations issued years ago would outweigh any informational gains from such an analysis. The comparison is crude because it gives equal weight to debt incurred during the considered year whether incurred at the beginning or end of the year. For the latter reason, calculations for some states whose debt changed radically during the year under consideration are unreliable and are not included. The crudeness is compounded because the calculations do not account for other compositional differences, such as average maturity of the debts, the credit rating of the states, and the year of original issue. Nonetheless, the results of this comparison seem of sufficient interest to present here, bearing in mind the limitations of the measures.

The results of the calculations for 1958 are shown in Table 13. They show a definite tendency for the states with a large percentage of state debt in nonguaranteed form to have higher interest costs than states with relatively little nonguaranteed debt. Using Spearman's formula for rank order correlation, a correlation coefficient of 0.744 was obtained from the rank relationship between the percentage of state debt in nonguaranteed form and the interest cost. This coefficient is highly significant and indicates that the tendency for states with higher proportions of total debt in nonguaranteed form to have higher interest costs is due to other than random causes.

TABLE 13

Interest cost on state debt compared with the composition
of state debt outstanding during 1958

State	Interest cost (per cent) plus ranking[a]	Percentage of state debt in nonguaranteed form plus ranking[b]	State	Interest cost (per cent) plus ranking[a]	Percentage of state debt in nonguaranteed form plus ranking[b]
Ala.	3.14 (30)	66 (22)	Mont.	3.18 (31)	86 (31)
Ariz.	2.83 (21)	100 (34)	Neb.	3.39 (38)	100 (34)
Ark.	3.05 (27)	20 (9)	Nev.	2.67 (16)	0 (1)
Calif.	2.56 (14)	8 (7)	N.H.	2.08 (3)	1 (4)
Colo.	3.02 (24)	100 (34)	N.J.	2.99 (23)	57 (20)
Del.	1.91 (1)	20 (9)	N.M.	2.34 (10)	48 (17)
Fla.	3.67 (41)	100 (34)	N.Y.	2.82 (20)	39 (14)
Ga.	3.46 (39)	100 (34)	N.C.	2.32 (8)	2 (5)
Idaho	2.74 (17)	68 (23)	Ohio	2.98 (22)	79 (29)
Ill.	3.03 (26)	71 (26)	Okla.	3.29 (36)	81 (30)
Ind.	3.35 (37)	100 (34)	Ore.	2.09 (4)	0 (1)
Iowa	2.12 (5)	39 (14)	Pa.	2.47 (12)	76 (28)
Kan.	3.50 (40)	100 (34)	R.I.	2.50 (13)	4 (6)
Ky.	3.02 (24)	52 (19)	S.C.	2.17 (6)	24 (11)
La.	3.09 (28)	30 (13)	Tex.	3.09 (28)	44 (16)
Me.	3.22 (34)	72 (27)	Utah	3.21 (33)	100 (34)
Md.	2.32 (8)	65 (21)	Vt.	2.05 (2)	0 (1)
Mass.	2.43 (11)	24 (11)	Va.	3.23 (35)	95 (33)
Mich.	2.81 (18)	69 (24)	Wash.	2.81 (18)	87 (32)
Minn.	2.21 (7)	9 (8)	W.Va.	3.19 (32)	51 (18)
Miss.	2.63 (15)	69 (24)			

[a] Rankings are in parentheses, e.g., state ranked no. 1 has the lowest interest cost.

[b] Rankings are in parentheses, e.g., states ranked no. 1 have the lowest percentage of total state debt in nonguaranteed form.

Source: Bureau of the Census, *Compendium of State Government Finances*, 1957 and 1958.

Note: These figures were calculated from data relating to state debt outstanding at the beginning and end of 1958 and interest payments during that year.

Interest Costs on Recent State Obligations

Data collected and made available by the Investment Bankers Association of America have enabled a more precise analysis of interest costs on state bonds issued during the period 1956–1959. Among the data collected by the IBA on state bond issues are: state and issuing agency; amount; date of issue; type of issue (various types of revenue bonds and general obligations); Moody's rating; average maturity; call provisions; purpose of issue; maturity provisions (term or serial); coupon rates; purchase price; and net interest cost to the issuing agency. From these data Tables 14–19 were prepared.

Gaps in the data made some approximations necessary. Net interest cost was not available for all of the issues. Where coupon

TABLE 14

Amount and average interest cost of general obligations
and revenue bonds issued by states in 1957

State	General obligations		Revenue bonds	
	Amount (thousands)	Average interest cost (per cent)	Amount (thousands)	Average interest cost (per cent)
Ala			$ 24,000	3.70
Calif.	$300,000	3.49		
Colo.			16,000	3.23
Conn.	64,153	3.16	115,000	4.06
Fla.			72,850	4.19
Ga.			51,000	4.03
Idaho			200	3.35
Ill.			3,750	4.35
Kan.			19,500	4.41
Ky.	35,000	2.97	250	4.43
La.	24,400	3.35	12,948	3.72
Md.	27,351	3.35		
Mass.	30,350	3.49		
Mich.			52,070	3.26
Miss.	15,550	3.17	2,500	3.19
Mo.	20,000	2.39		
Neb.			8,000	4.01
N.M.			4,000	2.63
N.Y.	64,425	2.75	6,800	3.78
N.C.	9,000	2.83		
Ohio	85,000	2.85	134,500	3.41
Ore.	52,300	3.33		
Pa.			36,600	3.72
R.I.	26,700	3.41		
S.C.	21,000	2.95		
S.D.			59	4.00
Tenn.	8,500	3.00		
Tex.	12,500	2.70	10,350	3.97
Wash.			95,200	4.29
Total	$796,229	——	$665,577	——
Average		3.22		3.78

Note: These figures were calculated from unpublished data on state bond issues made available by the Investment Bankers Association of America.

rates were known, the average coupon rate was used in place of an unknown net interest cost. In some cases neither the coupon rate nor the net interest cost was known; those issues were omitted from the calculations and are not included in the amount columns. For this reason, plus the fact that data on privately negotiated loans and loans from the federal government were not available, the amounts listed in the tables will not agree with Bureau of the Census figures on new state debt. The amounts shown in the tables include only issues for which interest cost data were avail-

TABLE 15

Amount and average interest cost of general obligations
and revenue bonds issued by states in 1958

State	General obligations		Revenue bonds	
	Amount (thousands)	Average interest cost (per cent)	Amount (thousands)	Average interest cost (per cent)
Ala.	$ 17,000	3.07		
Ariz.			$ 200	3.44
Calif.	400,000	3.21		
Colo.			5,000	2.66
Conn.	77,000	3.26		
Fla.			30,657	3.69
Ga.			55,920	3.75
Ill.			66,675	4.93
Ind.			36,500	4.23
Iowa	24,700	2.50		
Kan.			500	3.96
Ky.	35,000	3.00	141	2.87
La.	12,000	3.26	8,350	3.73
Md.	27,657	3.08		
Mass.	90,877	2.97	1,400	3.89
Mich.			103,000	3.33
Miss.	22,700	2.61	4,000	3.52
Mo.	55,000	2.34		
N.H.			355	4.12
N.M.			3,210	3.15
N.Y.	226,000	2.64		
N.C.	25,000	2.61		
Ohio			155,000	2.84
Okla.			175	4.13
Ore.	25,226	2.95		
Pa.			92,075	3.39
R.I.	11,750	3.15		
S.C.	46,000	2.47		
S.D.			30	4.00
Tenn.	15,000	2.69		
Tex.	25,325	2.92	50,761	2.75
Vt.	11,506	2.20		
Va.			6,150	4.67
Wash.			17,735	3.53
W.Va.	18,740	2.69		
Wis.			3,965	3.90
Total	$1,166,481	——	$641,799	——
Average		2.99		3.47

Note: These figures were calculated from unpublished data on state bond issues made available by the Investment Bankers Association of America.

able and serve primarily to emphasize the significance of the average interest cost figures. The average interest cost in the tables is the average of the net interest cost of each issue in the categories weighted by the amount of the issue. In some circumstances use of an unweighted average might be justified; in this case, how-

TABLE 16

Amount and average interest cost of general obligations and
revenue bonds issued by states in 1959

State	General obligations		Revenue bonds	
	Amount (thousands)	Average interest cost (per cent)	Amount (thousands)	Average interest cost (per cent)
Ala.			$ 32,000	3.64
Calif.	$ 203,554	3.85	34,000	4.36
Colo.			6,000	3.37
Conn.	77,410	3.56	62,500	4.30
Del.	16,350	3.29		
Fla.			80,530	3.94
Idaho	500	3.37	325	4.00
Ill.			7,285	4.40
Ind.			1,500	4.10
Kan.	505	3.44	200	3.50
Ky.			3,300	4.05
La.	30,000	3.50	550	4.35
Me.	9,500	3.07		
Md.	15,908	3.25	26,986	3.98
Mass.	71,762	3.47	54,800	4.71
Mich.			75,000	4.04
Minn.	38,136	3.01		
Miss.	37,700	3.24	18,000	4.34
Mo.			80	3.87
Neb.	3,892	4.50		
N.H.	10,089	3.21		
N.J.	91,800	3.37		
N.Y.	105,125	3.42	587,500	4.20
N.C.	3,000	3.24		
Ohio	30,000	3.10	35,025	3.68
Ore.	62,805	3.25		
Pa.	120,000	3.40	76,000	3.68
S.C.	16,500	3.05		
Tenn.	15,000	3.28		
Tex.	10,355	3.54	13,710	3.59
Vt.	13,025	3.10		
Wash.	25,000	3.17	12,625	3.42
W.Va.	5,000	3.56	11,328	4.24
Wyo.			9,130	3.75
Total	$1,012,916	——	$1,148,374	——
Average		3.45		4.11

Note: These figures were calculated from unpublished data on state bond issues made available by the Investment Bankers Association of America.

ever, it was felt that the weighting would remove any illusory effects of small issues with widely divergent interest costs.

Tables 14–16 present the average interest cost on revenue bonds and general obligations issued by the various states in the years 1957, 1958, and 1959, respectively. Before looking closely at the tables, certain limitations that attach themselves to tables of this

TABLE 17

Amount and average interest cost of general obligations
and revenue bonds by purpose of issue in 1957

Purpose of issue	General obligations		Revenue bonds	
	Amount (thousands)	Average interest cost (per cent)	Amount (thousands)	Average interest cost (per cent)
Education	$152,364	3.34	$ 81,959	4.01
Elementary & secondary	133,677	3.37	52,000	4.00
College-unclassified	350	3.00	6,080	4.49
College-dormitories	16,637	2.97	22,709	3.86
College-assemblies			1,170	4.75
Other libraries	1,700	4.50		
Highways and bridges	$147,688	3.31	$491,750	3.83
Roads-nontoll	112,688	3.40	180,500	3.43
Roads-toll			250,250	3.84
Bridges-toll			61,000	4.87
Multipurpose	35,000	2.97		
Utilities	$ 6,000	3.36	$ 20,600	3.88
Water	5,000	3.25	5,800	3.82
Sewer	1,000	3.90		
Electric			8,000	4.01
Multipurpose			6,800	3.78
Public housing	$ 40,425	2.67		
State institutions	$ 42,475	2.86		
Mental	29,375	2.91		
Clinics	13,100	2.74		
Recreation	$ 750			
Parks and beaches	750			
Transportation	$ 25,750	3.36	$ 2,300	4.34
Port facilities	25,400	3.36		
Harbor and river			2,000	4.32
Other transportation	350	3.68	300	4.48
State buildings	$ 22,000	2.39	$ 28,048	3.77
Offices	22,000	2.39	28,048	3.77
Veterans' aid	$324,600	3.33	$ 1,000	3.39
Flood control	$ 7,982			
Other unclassified	$ 38,200	2.82	$ 35,000	3.86

Note: These figures were calculated from unpublished data on state bond issues made available by the Investment Bankers Association of America.

type must be noted. Though the tables are three-way classifications, certain variables which might affect the average interest cost are not considered. Differences between the average interest cost are not solely due to being general obligations or revenue bonds, as the tables might imply. The time of the year the securities were issued, the average maturity of the issues, and call provisions are variables which might mitigate some of the differential, or for that matter hide a greater differential. For the most part, states issued one type of obligation or the other. Comparisons

TABLE 18

Amount and average interest cost of general obligations and
revenue bonds by purpose of issue in 1958

Purpose of issue	General obligations		Revenue bonds	
	Amount (thousands)	Average interest cost (per cent)	Amount (thousands)	Average interest cost (per cent)
Education	$248,066	3.16	$ 86,341	3.74
Elementary & secondary	173,790	3.04	21,220	3.67
College-unclassified	67,751	3.46	48,500	3.68
College-dormitories	3,525	3.25	7,621	3.99
College-assemblies	1,500	3.37	2,270	3.83
College-athl. buildings			6,730	4.23
College-libraries	1,500			
Highways and bridges	$379,157	2.94	$392,015	3.45
Roads-nontoll	207,157	2.80	290,465	3.15
Roads-toll	127,000	3.20	90,150	4.43
Bridges-nontoll	10,000	2.50	6,200	3.98
Bridges-toll			5,200	2.97
Multipurpose	35,000	3.00		
Utilities	$ 11,927	2.98	$ 11,520	4.39
Water	4,607	3.00	4,155	5.09
Sewer	7,320	2.97		
Water and sewer			7,365	4.00
Public housing	$ 49,000	2.92		
State institutions	$ 8,700	2.67	$ 3,000	3.09
Hospitals	8,700	2.67	3,000	3.09
Recreation	$ 2,000	3.00	$ 75	5.25
Parks and beaches			75	5.25
Recreation centers	2,000	3.00		
Transportation	$ 22,975	2.81	$ 4,270	3.95
Port facilities	18,475	2.73	4,220	3.96
Harbor and river	3,000	3.31		
Airports	1,500		50	3.75
State buildings	$ 60,910	2.37	$ 38,285	4.16
Offices	60,585	2.37	34,310	4.16
Armories	325			
Penal			3,700	
Parking facilities			275	4.03
Veterans' aid	$331,540	3.02	$ 6,000	3.46
Flood control	$ 8,200	3.00		
Other unclassified	$ 37,850	3.06	$ 60,000	3.03

Note: These figures were calculated from unpublished data on state bond issues made available by the Investment Bankers Association of America.

between the revenue bonds of one state and the general obligations of another state are affected by the credit rating of those states. To the extent that one state has issued both types, one can assume a constant credit rating with little loss of accuracy. There are many types of securities included within the category revenue bonds; the tables present only an average of all revenue bond types and hence hide any differences among those alternative types.

TABLE 19

Amount and average interest cost of general obligations and
revenue bonds by purpose of issue in 1959

Purpose of issue	General obligations		Revenue bonds	
	Amount (thousands)	Average interest cost (per cent)	Amount (thousands)	Average interest cost (per cent)
Education	$258,502	3.44	$ 65,671	3.99
Elementary & secondary	119,647	3.54	7,530	4.00
College-unclassified	137,350	3.35	38,930	3.85
College-dormitories	1,505	3.16	6,745	4.05
College-assemblies			5,603	4.35
College-athl. buildings			2,838	4.03
Other libraries			4,025	4.78
Highways and bridges	$136,200	3.22	$409,936	4.12
Roads-nontoll	127,200	3.23	199,136	3.86
Roads-toll			115,000	4.17
Bridges-nontoll			2,000	4.43
Bridges-toll			93,800	4.67
Multipurpose	9,000	3.07		
Utilities	$ 59,698	3.39	$400,000	4.21
Water	45,698	3.37		
Sewer	13,500	3.46		
Electric			400,000	4.21
Transit	500	3.07		
Public housing	$ 55,125	3.48		
State institutions	$ 36,000	3.14		
Mental	36,000	3.14		
Recreation	$ 1,546	4.16		
Parks and beaches	1,546	4.16		
Transportation	$ 2,500	3.16	$ 2,000	4.98
Port facilities	2,000	3.15	2,000	4.98
Airports	500	3.22		
State buildings	$ 28,700	3.16	$ 11,375	3.35
Offices	28,700	3.16	11,375	3.35
Veterans' aid	$323,250	3.55		
Flood control	$ 7,800	3.26		
Other unclassified	$171,493	3.36	$ 62,400	3.71

Note: These figures were calculated from unpublished data on state bond issues made available by the Investment Bankers Association of America.

As will be indicated in Tables 17–19, the purpose of the state issues may have an effect on the interest cost of the issues. In short, by presenting averages and ignoring other variables the tables do not present the whole picture. I will attempt to make some sense out of this mass of variables in the Technical Note to this chapter.

For now, let us consider the results in Tables 14–16. With two exceptions, the average interest cost of revenue bonds exceeded the average interest cost of general obligations where states issued both types of bonds during the same year. The two exceptions, Kentucky and Texas in 1958, can be readily explained. Kentucky's one revenue issue of $141,000 in 1958 had an average maturity of eight years, while its one general obligation issue of $35 million had an average maturity of twenty-three years. This factor more than accounts for the differential of 0.13 per cent shown in Table 15. The revenue bonds issued in Texas during 1958 were for the most part highly secure limited tax bonds of state colleges with very short maturities ranging from four to six years, while the important general obligations issued had maturities of nineteen and twenty years. For all states combined the average interest cost of revenue bonds exceeded the average interest cost of general obligations by 0.56 per cent, 0.48 per cent, and 0.66 per cent in 1957, 1958, and 1959, respectively.

Tables 17, 18, and 19 present the average cost on revenue bonds and general obligations issued by all states for various purposes in 1957, 1958, and 1959, respectively. These tables contain limitations similar to those applied to Tables 14–16. Being only three-way classifications, the tables do not account for the effect of variables not included in the classification. Differences between the cells in the tables are not solely due to differences in bond types or purpose of issue, but may also be due to such differences as the credit rating of the issuing state and maturity of the issues. Nevertheless, it is felt that the results are of sufficient interest to present here. In every case the average interest cost of revenue bonds exceeded the average interest cost of general obligations issued for a similar purpose during the same year.

Statistical Estimation of the Interest Cost Differential Between Revenue Bonds and General Obligations

While average interest cost differentials may be interesting, they do not provide adequate means of estimating the interest cost differential between revenue bonds and general obligations under any given set of circumstances. Use of averages does not permit control of variables which affect the cost of issuing bonds. The fund of data supplied by the Investment Bankers Association has enabled the application of statistical estimation to this problem. Using the technique of multiple regression, estimates of the interest cost of issuing revenue bonds and general obligations can be made for varying conditions of maturity, purpose, etc. The added interest cost of a particular revenue bond issue can then be derived by comparing the estimated interest cost of that issue with the estimated interest cost of general obligations issued under similar circumstances. This method of estimation gives rather nice results because variables affecting the interest cost of state borrowing can be controlled in the estimating process. (The statistical techniques are outlined in the Technical Note to this chapter.)

Tables 20–23 contain estimates of the added interest cost of issuing revenue bonds under various possible conditions. Table 20 gives estimates of the added interest cost of issuing revenue bonds over general obligations for construction of a toll road under various circumstances of credit rating, maturity, and general level of interest rates at the date of issue. Table 21, 22, and 23, respectively, give similar estimates for the added cost of revenue financing of utilities; of purposes other than utilities or toll roads and bridges where rental revenue from the state is used as security for the revenue issue; and for purposes other than utilities or toll roads and bridges where other than rental revenue

TABLE 20

Estimates of the added interest cost of revenue bonds
issued for toll roads and bridges

Average maturity (years)	Long-term government bond yield at date of issue					
	3.00 per cent			4.00 per cent		
	Moody's rating[a]			Moody's rating[a]		
	Aaa–Aa	Aa–A	A–Baa	Aaa–Aa	Aa–A	A–Baa
5	0.5616	0.7086	0.6240	0.6053	0.7523	0.6677
10	0.5701	0.7171	0.6325	0.6138	0.7608	0.6762
15	0.5786	0.7256	0.6410	0.6223	0.7693	0.6847
20	0.5871	0.7341	0.6495	0.6308	0.7778	0.6932
25	0.5956	0.7426	0.6580	0.6393	0.7863	0.7017
30	0.6041	0.7511	0.6665	0.6478	0.7948	0.7102
35	0.6126	0.7596	0.6750	0.6563	0.8033	0.7187
40	0.6211	0.7681	0.6835	0.6648	0.8118	0.7272

[a] The first rating applies to general obligations and the second to comparable revenue bonds, e.g., states issuing general obligations rated Aaa would have a rating of Aa on revenue bonds; hence, Aaa–Aa, Aa–A, A–Baa.

Note: These figures were calculated from equations (7), (8), and (9) in the Technical Note to this chapter. Calculations are based upon callable general obligations.

TABLE 21

Estimates of the added interest cost of revenue bonds issued for utilities

Average Maturity (years)	Long-term government bond yield at date of issue					
	3.00 per cent			4.00 per cent		
	Moody's rating[a]			Moody's rating[a]		
	Aaa–Aa	Aa–A	A–Baa	Aaa–Aa	Aa–A	A–Baa
5	0.6261	0.7731	0.6885	0.6698	0.8168	0.7322
10	0.6346	0.7816	0.6970	0.6783	0.8253	0.7407
15	0.6431	0.7901	0.7055	0.6868	0.8338	0.7492
20	0.6516	0.7986	0.7140	0.6953	0.8423	0.7577
25	0.6601	0.8071	0.7225	0.7038	0.8508	0.7662
30	0.6686	0.8156	0.7310	0.7123	0.8593	0.7747
35	0.6771	0.8241	0.7395	0.7208	0.8678	0.7832
40	0.6856	0.8326	0.7480	0.7293	0.8763	0.7917

[a] The first rating applies to general obligations and the second to comparable revenue bonds, e.g., states issuing general obligations rated Aaa would have a rating of Aa on revenue bonds; hence, Aaa–Aa, Aa–A, A–Baa.

Note: These figures were calculated from equations (7), (8), and (9) in the Technical Note to this chapter. Calculations are based upon callable general obligations.

TABLE 22

Estimates of the added interest cost of revenue bonds issued for purposes other than toll roads and bridges or utilities, and secured by rental revenue from the state

Average maturity (years)	Long-term government bond yield at date of issue					
	3.00 per cent			4.00 per cent		
	Moody's rating[a]			Moody's rating[a]		
	Aaa–Aa	Aa–A	A–Baa	Aaa–Aa	Aa–A	A–Baa
5	0.4710	0.5640	0.4794	0.4607	0.6077	0.5231
10	0.4255	0.5725	0.4879	0.4692	0.6162	0.5316
15	0.4340	0.5810	0.4964	0.4777	0.6247	0.5401
20	0.4425	0.5895	0.5049	0.4862	0.6332	0.5486
25	0.4510	0.5980	0.5134	0.4947	0.6417	0.5571
30	0.4595	0.6065	0.5219	0.5032	0.6502	0.5656
35	0.4680	0.6150	0.5304	0.5117	0.6587	0.5741
40	0.4765	0.6235	0.5489	0.5202	0.6672	0.5826

[a] The first rating applies to general obligations and the second to comparable revenue bonds, e.g., states issuing general obligations rated Aaa would have a rating of Aa on revenue bonds; hence, Aaa–Aa, Aa–A, A–Baa.

Note: These figures were calculated from equations (7), (8), and (9) in the Technical Note to this chapter. Calculations are based upon callable general obligations.

TABLE 23

Estimates of the added interest cost of revenue bonds issued for purposes other
than toll roads and bridges or utilities, and secured by other
than rental revenue from the state

Average maturity (years)	Long-term government bond yield at date of issue					
	3.00 per cent			4.00 per cent		
	Moody's rating[a]			Moody's rating[a]		
	Aaa–Aa	Aa–A	A–Baa	Aaa–Aa	Aa–A	A–Baa
5	0.2907	0.4377	0.3531	0.3344	0.4814	0.3968
10	0.2992	0.4462	0.3616	0.3429	0.4899	0.4053
15	0.3077	0.4547	0.3701	0.3514	0.4984	0.4138
20	0.3162	0.4632	0.3786	0.3599	0.5069	0.4223
25	0.3247	0.4717	0.3871	0.3684	0.5154	0.4308
30	0.3332	0.4802	0.3956	0.3769	0.5239	0.4393
35	0.3417	0.4887	0.4041	0.3854	0.5324	0.4478
40	0.3502	0.4972	0.4126	0.3939	0.5409	0.4563

[a] The first rating applies to general obligations and the second to comparable revenue bonds, e.g., states issuing general obligations rated Aaa would have a rating of Aa on revenue bonds; hence, Aaa-Aa, Aa-A, A-Baa.

Note: These figures were calculated from equations (7), (8), and (9) in the Technical Note to this chapter. Calculations are based upon callable general obligations.

acts as security for the revenue issue. These categories were employed because they account for the purposes of revenue bond issues and the types of security that proved to be significant determinants of the interest cost on revenue bond issues.[2]

The estimates were further based on the presumption that state general obligations would carry a higher credit rating than revenue issues of the same state. For example, in the second and fifth columns of Tables 20–23 the estimates were based on the assumption that the issuing state could issue general obligations carrying a credit rating of Aaa, but revenue bonds of that same state would carry a rating of Aa. This presumption is based on the observation that states which issued both types of bonds more often than not had a credit rating attached to their general obligations which was one notch higher than the rating fixed to their revenue bonds. Comparative ratings for states issuing both types of bonds during the period 1957–1959 are shown in Table 24.

Specific estimates would be made from Tables 20–23 in the following manner. Suppose a state considers building a toll road to be financed by either (1) issuing 40-year, callable general obligations, or (2) establishing a public authority which will issue

TABLE 24

Moody's credit ratings on general obligations and revenue bonds where both types
of obligations have been issued by the same state during the period 1957–1959[a]

| State | Typical rating | |
	General obligations	Revenue bonds
Conn.	Aaa	A
Calif.	Aa	A
Ky.	Aa	A
La.	A	A
Md.[b]	Aaa	Aa
Mass.	Aa	A
Miss.	Aa	A
Ohio	Aaa	Aa
Pa.	Aa	Aa–A[c]
Tex.	Aa	Aaa–Baa[d]
Wash.	Aa	A

[a] Some states which have issued both types of bonds during this period have been omitted, because Moody's did not rate the revenue bonds.
[b] 1958–1959.
[c] Three issues rated Aa and three rated A.
[d] Seven issues rated Aaa and three rated Baa.
Source: Investment Bankers Association (unpublished data).

40-year revenue bonds.[3] The amount required is $100 million and the general level of interest rates, typified by the yield on long-term government bonds, is expected to be 3.00 per cent on the date of issue. This state typically has a credit rating of Aa attached to its general obligations. The estimated differential between the interest cost of the two types of financing can be found by going to Table 20, column three (under a long-term government bond yield of 3.00 per cent and a Moody's rating of Aa-A) down to the row for maturities of 40 years. The estimated added interest cost of financing by method (2), revenue bonds, over method (1), general obligations, is 0.7681 per cent. On an issue of $100 million the added yearly cost of servicing the revenue bonds would be $768,000, and the added cost over the life of the issue would be $30,120,000.

An estimate of the added interest cost of financing a $5,000,000 state office building via a lease-purchase agreement with a state building authority, state rental revenue to act as security for the bonds, would be obtained in Table 22. Assuming that the authority would issue serial bonds with an average maturity of 25 years, a long-term government bond yield of 4.00 per cent at the date of issue, and that a credit rating of Aaa would be attached to general obligations of the state, the estimated added interest cost would be 0.4947 per cent. The yearly added cost of servicing the bonds would be $24,735, and the added cost over the life of the issue would be $618,375.

Estimates of the added cost of revenue financing under various other circumstances would be similarly made. Estimates for maturities and government bond yields other than those in the tables can be made by interpolation.

Added Interest Costs Quantified in Selected States

Statistical techniques also make possible a more precise estimation of the added costs incurred by specific states which have issued revenue bonds. Although estimates have been made as to the added costs of particular state issues,[4] no comprehensive studies are available which have quantified these added costs on all state issues, thereby dramatizing the effect of constitutional debt limitations on total state interest payments. That will be done in this section for Alabama, Georgia, Illinois, Indiana, Pennsylvania, Washington, and Wisconsin, for all debt issued between July 1, 1956, and December 31, 1959.

The basic procedure is simple. It involves a comparison of the actual interest cost on a state's revenue bonds with the estimated interest cost of comparable general obligations that might have been issued by that state. The major difficulty lies in the estimation of this latter interest cost. Prior studies have estimated the added cost of particular state revenue bonds by using average yields on municipal general obligations as an estimate of the interest cost of comparable general obligations.[5] Such estimates by their very nature are rather crude. For this study more precise estimates have been made by applying the techniques of multiple regression to the data gathered by the Investment Bankers Association. The statistical procedures are outlined in detail in the Technical Note to this chapter, but some general considerations must be noted at this point for a better understanding of what has been done.

The object is to estimate the interest cost of general obligations in such a manner that any determined interest differentials (between revenue bonds and their general obligation counterparts) are due solely to the nature of the bonds as revenue bonds or general obligations. This can be accomplished only by estimating the interest cost that would have been paid on general obligations similar in all other respects, such as maturity, date of issue, and call provisions. This is where the use of average yields on municipal general obligations fails. The estimates used here have been based on a regression equation which states that the interest cost on a particular state general obligation is a function of the general level of interest rates at the date of issue, the average maturity of the issue, the call provisions, and the credit rating of the state.

Because the rating services apparently rate revenue bonds on a different basis than they rate general obligations, the credit rating applied to the hypothetical general obligation may differ from the actual rating given a state on its revenue bonds. If a state has issued general obligations in the past, the rating generally applied thereto has been used; if no such rating is available, a rating one notch above the rating on the revenue bonds was used. As noted in the previous section, the latter method can be justified by the general observation that the ratings applied to revenue bonds tend to average one notch lower where states have issued both types of obligations. Other variables were considered but, as will be shown in the Technical Note, those variables do not prove to be significant determinants of the interest cost on state general obligations.

In a few cases the estimated interest cost of general obligations exceeded the interest cost of their revenue counterparts. This, of course, might be expected because of the nature of statistical estimation. In those cases negative interest differentials were not considered, because it was felt that generally the state could have guaranteed the bonds without having to pay the higher rate. It was assumed that the unusually low interest cost on the revenue bonds was due to unknown factors that would have similarly lowered the cost of comparable general obligations.

The foregoing provided the basis upon which were made calculations of the added interest payments attributed to the issuance of revenue bonds in the selected states during the period 1956–1959. It is estimated that Alabama has annual interest payments of $181,800 more than it would have had with full-faith and credit financing. This added amount will diminish after 1968 as the issues mature. Again it must be pointed out that the calculations do not include figures for debt issued prior to 1956 which would tend to raise the amount of the added interest payments wherever revenue bonds had been so issued, and were still outstanding in 1960. It must also be assumed that revenue bonds issued after 1959 will contribute to this amount.

With similar qualifications, estimates show that the added annual interest payments in the six other states are: Georgia, $720,000; Illinois, $976,055; Indiana, $415,997; Pennsylvania, $496,061; Washington, $1,054,212; and Wisconsin, $117,659. The breakdown of the revenue bonds, hypothetical interest rates on comparable general obligations, and the resulting added interest payments for the selected states are shown in Tables 25–31. The breakdown includes only revenue bonds issued to private investors. Information about privately negotiated loans secured by revenue-producing state projects, with the exception of Wisconsin, was not available and hence not included. Loans made to the states by the federal goverement were also not included, because the interest charged by the federal lending agencies was well below the market rate of interest, amounting to a subsidy for the state projects.

TABLE 25

Estimated additional interest costs from revenue bond financing
in Alabama from 1956 to 1959

Date of issue (month and year)	Amount of issue (thousands)	Average maturity (years)	Interest cost (per cent)	Interest cost of similar general obs.[a] (per cent)	Added annual interest payments	Added payments over life of issue
12–56	$ 4,000	14	4.00	3.33	$ 26,800	$ 375,200
1–57	6,000	13	3.69	3.24	27,000	351,000
2–57	4,000	18	3.98	3.30	27,200	489,600
3–57	14,000	12	3.63	3.16	65,800	789,600
4–59	20,000	11	3.41	3.65		
9–59	2,000	9	4.98	3.76	24,000	216,000
11–59	10,000	11	3.83	3.72	11,000	121,000
Total	$60,000				$181,800	$2,342,400

[a] Calculated from equation (7) in the Technical Note to this chapter.
Note: Data on revenue bonds, columns 1–4, were taken from the data of the Investment Bankers Association of America described in the text of this chapter.

TABLE 26
Estimated additional interest costs from revenue bond financing
in Georgia from 1956 to 1959

Date of issue (month and year)	Amount of issue (thousands)	Average maturity (years)	Interest cost (per cent)	Interest cost of similar general obs.[a] (per cent)	Added annual interest payments	Added payments over life of issue
1–57	$17,500	9	3.81	2.91	$157,500	$1,417,500
2–57	10,000	15	4.03	2.99	104,000	1,560,000
7–57	17,500	10	4.08	3.11	169,750	1,697,500
10–57	6,000	14	4.50	3.31	71,400	999,600
1–58	17,500	15	3.41	3.00	71,750	1,076,250
8–58	21,000	16	3.72	3.28	92,400	1,478,400
9–58	6,200	15	3.98	3.35	39,060	585,900
11–58	930	16	4.00	3.35	6,045	96,720
11–58	1,290	16	4.00	3.35	8,385	134,160
Total	$97,920				$720,290	$9,046,030

[a] Calculated from equation (7) in the Technical Note to this chapter.
Note: Data on revenue bonds, columns 1–4, were taken from the data of the Investment Bankers Association of America described in the text of this chapter.

TABLE 27
Estimated additional interest costs from revenue bond financing
in Illinois from 1956 to 1959

Date of issue (month and year)	Amount of issue (thousands)	Average maturity (years)	Interest cost (per cent)	Interest cost of similar general obs.[a] (per cent)	Added annual interest payments	Added payments over life of issue
9–56	$ 320	9	3.95	2.81	$ 3,868	$ 34,812
11–56	2,250	26	4.85	3.34	33,975	883,350
3–57	3,750	26	3.77	3.22	5,500	143,000
4–58	64,000	40	4.97	3.60	876,800	35,072,000
11–58	1,625	19	3.94	3.43	8,287	157,453
3–59	3,600	26	4.26	3.77	17,640	458,640
3–59	625	22	4.38	3.66	4,500	99,000
6–59	110	5	4.22	3.32	990	4,950
9–59	3,450	19	4.52	3.81	24,495	465,405
Total	$79,730				$976,055	$37,318,610

[a] Calculated from equation (7) in the Technical Note to this chapter.
Note: Data on revenue bonds, columns 1–4, were taken from the data of the Investment Bankers Association of America described in the text of this chapter.

TABLE 28

Estimated additional interest costs from revenue bond financing
in Indiana from 1956 to 1959

Date of issue (month and year)	Amount of issue (thousands)	Average maturity (years)	Interest cost (per cent)	Interest cost of similar general obs.ᵃ (per cent)	Added annual interest payments	Added payments over life of issue
10–56	$ 2,985	24	4.12	3.11	$ 30,148	$ 723,552
10–56	6,065	35	4.25	3.41	51,114	1,788,990
10–56	3,350	11	3.87	2.76	37,185	409,035
8–58	6,500	18	4.25	3.33	59,800	1,076,400
9–58	30,000	19	4.22	3.46	228,000	4,332,000
6–59	1,500	10	4.10	3.45	9,750	97,500
Total	$50,400				$415,997	$8,427,477

ᵃ Calculated from equation (7) in the Technical Note to this chapter.
Note: Data on revenue bonds, columns 1–4, were taken from the data of the Investment
Bankers Association of America described in the text of this chapter.

TABLE 29

Estimated additional interest costs from revenue bond financing
in Pennsylvania from 1956 to 1959

Date of issue (month and year)	Amount of issue (thousands)	Average maturity (years)	Interest cost (per cent)	Interest cost of similar general obs.ᵃ (per cent)	Added annual interest payments	Added payments over life of issue
8–56	$ 13,750	20	3.00	3.08	$	$
1–57	800	27	4.27	3.39	7,040	190,080
9–57	25,000	14	3.79	3.26	132,500	1,855,000
1–58	8,710	41	3.90	3.71	16,549	678,509
1–58	20,000	12	2.63	2.92		
4–58	8,950	22	4.00	3.11	79,655	1,752,410
4–58	9,050	22	4.00	3.11	80,545	1,771,990
5–58	7,000	41	3.70	3.64	4,200	172,200
7–58	30,000	14	3.34	3.06	84,000	1,176,000
9–58	175	40	4.50	3.03	2,572	102,880
3–59	30,000	14	3.58	3.44	42,000	588,000
6–59	10,000	11	3.55	3.48	7,000	77,000
10–59	25,000	15	3.76	3.60	40,000	600,000
Total	$188,435				$496,061	$8,964,069

ᵃ Calculated from equation (7) in the Technical Note to this chapter.
Note: Data on revenue bonds, columns 1–4, were taken from the data of the Investment
Bankers Association of America described in the text of this chapter.

TABLE 30

Estimated additional interest costs from revenue bond financing
in Washington from 1956 to 1959

Date of issue (month and year)	Amount of issue (thousands)	Average maturity (years)	Interest cost (per cent)	Interest cost of similar general obs.[a] (per cent)	Added annual interest payments	Added payments over life of issue
8–56	$ 1,750	9	3.24	2.78	$ 8,050	$ 72,450
9–56	5,375	31	4.46	3.40	56,975	1,766,225
3–57	1,000	7	3.39	2.71	6,800	47,600
5–57	10,000	12	3.71	3.03	68,000	816,000
10–57	52,000	9	4.00	3.08	478,000	4,302,000
11–57	30,000	40	5.00	3.90	335,000	13,400,000
2–58	2,350	10	3.83	2.88	22,325	223,250
4–58	5,200	10	2.97	2.79	9,360	93,600
7–58	185	18	3.82	3.17	1,202	21,636
9–58	10,000	10	3.74	3.22	52,000	520,000
2–59	9,875	10	3.24	3.33		
4–59	2,750	12	4.05	3.45	16,500	198,000
Total	$130,485				$1,054,212	$21,460,761

[a] Calculated from equation (7) in the Technical Note to this chapter.
Note: Data on revenue bonds, columns 1–4, were taken from the data of the Investment Bankers Association of America described in the text of this chapter.

TABLE 31

Estimated additional interest costs from revenue bond financing
in Wisconsin from 1956 to 1959

Date of issue (month and year)	Amount of issue (thousands)	Average maturity (years)	Interest cost (per cent)	Interest cost of similar general obs.[a] (per cent)	Added annual interest payments	Added payments over life of issue
7–58	$ 3,430	23	4.00	3.07	$ 31,899	$ 733,677
9–58	8,325	17	3.87	3.18	55,842	949,314
12–59	10,685	17	3.91	3.63	29,918	508,606
Total	$22,440				$117,659	$2,191,597

[a] Calculated from equation (7) in the Technical Note to this chapter.
Note: Data on revenue bonds, columns 1–4, were taken from the data of the Investment Bankers Association of America described in the text of this chapter.

The foregoing estimates are of a partial nature and do not account for changes in the underlying structure of the interest costs applicable to revenue bonds and general obligations which would occur if most states ceased issuing revenue bonds. Presumably, the

rates on general obligations would rise and the rates on revenue
bonds would fall in this event, thereby narrowing the differential
between the two types of issues. Just how much the differential
would narrow would depend upon many imponderables, such as
how many revenue bond investors would be willing to accept lower
rates on general obligations, how many would switch to corporate
bonds, etc.

Significance of the Interest Rate Differential

Sufficient evidence has now been presented to prove the existence of a significant interest differential between guaranteed and
nonguaranteed borrowing. The next problem is to probe the economic significance of the differential. Revenue bonds carry higher
interest rates than comparable general obligations because of the
greater risk that accompanies revenue bonds. A political unit
which is free to use either type of obligation presumably would
issue revenue bonds when it wished to shift the risk of project
failure from the public to the lenders of funds. When that political
unit wishes to accept for the public the risk of project failure by
pledging general taxes, it will issue general obligations. In this
sense one can view the interest differential as a premium to induce revenue bondholders to accept the ultimate risk that any
given project will not live up to expectations.

If one could assume a rationality to the voting process in the
sense that the electorate could endow elected officials with a knowledge of their time preference and risk preference, the alternative
use of revenue bonds or general obligations would not determine
the amount of public investment expenditure. Consider the following example: a state considers alternative projects A, B, and
C. The estimated returns from projects A, B, and C are 5.0 per
cent, 4.0 per cent, and 3.0 per cent, respectively. In this first situation assume that the benefits from the three projects are primarily
direct and can be recovered by user charges on the public. Examples of this type of project might be harbor improvements,
water and power utilities, toll roads and bridges, and student
dormitories. The state can borrow funds at a cost of 3.5 per cent
by pledging the general funds of the state, that is, by issuing
general obligations. The state could finance project A by issuing

revenue bonds carrying a rate of 4.5 percent. Projects B and C could not be financed by revenue bonds, because the expected return is less than the cost of servicing the bonds. In this case the revenue bond purchasers demand a premium of 1.0 per cent to assume the risk that project A will not yield the expected return. The questions to be posed: (1) which projects will the state undertake? (2) which type of obligations will be issued?

Clearly the state could undertake projects B and C only by issuing general obligations; but project A could be undertaken by either method of financing. If the rationality assumption is invoked, then projects B and C would not be undertaken. This seems clear in the case of project C, because the expected return of 3.0 per cent is less than the capital cost of 3.5 per cent. The state would not undertake project B either, even though the capital cost of 3.5 per cent is less than the expected return of 4.0 per cent. In this case the fact that lenders of funds would not purchase revenue bonds issued for project B at the rate of 4.0 per cent indicates that the return on investments of comparable risk is greater than 4.0 per cent elsewhere in the economy; and a rational use of public funds would preclude undertaking project B. Project A would be undertaken because the expected return of 5.0 per cent is apparently greater than the return on comparably uncertain investments as shown by the willingness of lenders to purchase revenue bonds at a rate of 4.5 per cent. Which method of financing would be used depends on the risk preference of the electorate. If the public liked risk, the managers would float general obligations. If the public disliked risk, the managers would float revenue bonds.

Consider a second situation. Assume that the benefits to be realized from projects A, B, and C are substantially indirect and, for the most part, cannot or will not be recovered by user charges on the public. Examples of this type of project are prisons, welfare institutions, free roads, and public schools. Under these circumstances, revenue bonds would have to be serviced and secured with revenues generated from special taxes or state appropriations in the form of rentals. In this case the revenue bond purchasers will be primarily concerned with the expectation that the special taxes or state rentals will be sufficient to service the bonds. Only indirectly will the purchasers be concerned with the results of the project itself, and then only to the extent that the outcome of the project will affect the yield of the taxes or the state's willingness to continue rental appropriations.

Under the foregoing conditions, the state would have to estimate the risk that a project will not live up to expectations inasmuch as the market will fail to yield such an estimation. If it can be assumed that an unbiased estimate of risk can be made, and that this risk premium is 1.0 per cent on all three projects for purposes of this illustration; and, if rationality can be further assumed, then the same investment decisions would be made as in the first situation. Project A could be undertaken by either revenue bonds or general obligations, because the expected return of 5.0 per cent is greater than the return on comparably uncertain investments in other sectors of the economy as measured by the basic capital cost of 3.5 per cent on general obligations plus the estimated risk premium of 1.0 per cent. In this second situation, the state could undertake projects B and C with revenue bonds as well as with general obligations, because the revenues which service the bonds would come from other sources—special taxes or rentals—the yield of which may have no direct relation to the outcome of projects B and C. If rationality is invoked, however, the state would not undertake projects B and C by either method, because the returns of 4.0 per cent and 3.0 per cent are less than the return on alternative investments of comparable risk.

The point to be established by the foregoing illustration is that under assumptions of rationality public investment expenditures would be made only when the return on the investments, direct or indirect, equaled or exceeded the return on investments in other sectors of the economy. The free choice of public managers to issue revenue bonds or general obligations would not alter the investments to be made, but would merely enable the managers to accept risk for the public or shift risk to lenders of funds.

Most certainly the voting process in the various states does not generate the degree of rationality assumed above. At best, honest managers attempt to estimate the desires of the public on the multitude of issues that lead to the election of one candidate over another. Some would claim that public managers are basically "dishonest" in the sense that they embrace positions which appear most likely in the short run to keep them in office. For instance, they would claim that, if rationality is relaxed, managers in the first situation of the foregoing illustration would undertake projects B and C by issuing general obligations because the services thereby rendered would create a favorable short-run illusion that the managers had done something "good" for the people. In this case, foreclosing the right of public managers to issue general obligations by constitutional provision would prevent the incurring of debt for unsound public projects. Leaving the door open for revenue bonds would enable the managers to undertake projects which were sound enough to yield the return necessary to induce lenders of funds to assume the risk by their purchase of revenue bonds.

This position is only tenable, however, if projects are financed solely with revenue bonds serviced and secured by user charges on the public for services of those projects. Once revenue bonds of the type in situation two above are adopted, public managers can borrow for unsound projects by pledging revenues from sources other than user charges on beneficiaries of the projects. If states can issue general obligations to finance economically unwise projects, then they can also issue revenue bonds to finance similarly unwise projects merely by pledging special taxes or state rental appropriations. As it stands today, "dishonest" managers in debt-limit states can undertake public projects by issuing revenue bonds where the real benefit may be substantially less than the capital cost.

In this area of public psychology one can seldom make definitive conclusions as to the rational nature of the voting process or the political honesty or dishonesty of public managers. The evidence presented in Chapter 3 seems to indicate that managers at the state level in states unrestricted in borrowing matters have not been much if any more dishonest than managers in restricted states; all of which might indicate that public managers in general are not dishonest at all. The experience of the various groups of states in borrowing matters may indicate that a degree of voting rationality does in fact exist.

Constitutional restrictions tend to frustrate public freedom to accept risk collectively by the issuance of general obligations for public projects. These restrictions force the borrowing public to shift the risk to lenders of funds via the use of revenue bonds and, consequently, pay the higher rate that risk requires. There may be institutional reasons why the public desires to accept the risk of the failure of its enterprises in spite of constitutional restrictions. This would be reflected in a willingness to appropriate tax funds, or otherwise assume debt, in the event of a public enterprise failure. This willingness might arise from public pride, or from a general aversion to the stigma of a bad credit rating. To the extent that constitutional debt restrictions prevent states from making this willingness known to its lenders, the public may wind up voluntarily accepting the risk and yet paying the risk premium to lenders of funds.

If a state were a closed economy, the result would merely be a shift in the allocation of income between risk lovers and risk haters; but states are open, and the result would be a flow of funds out of a restricted state to lenders in other states. Wisconsin residents may be paying New York lenders a rate on borrowed funds based on a greater risk than in reality exists. This hiatus between the apparent risk and real risk may result in a real cost of borrowing funds via the revenue bond method, where such borrowing is required by the presence of constitutional restrictions against state debt.

TECHNICAL NOTE TO CHAPTER 4

This note is devoted to the development of a statistical model by which the interest cost differential between revenue bonds and general obligations may be estimated. The data used in the following regression analyses are the data, made available by the Investment Bankers Association, which have been previously described in the body of the chapter.

The model revolves around the following relationships:

$$I_g = f(R, A, P, C, M, L), \tag{1}$$

and

$$I_r = g(T, R, A, P, S, C, B, M, L), \tag{2}$$

where

I_g = the interest cost of state general obligations,

I_r = the interest cost of state and state authority revenue bonds.

T = the type of issuer, state or state authority,

R = the credit rating of the issuer,

A = the amount of the issue,

P = the purpose of the issue,

S = the security for the issue,

C = the call provisions,

B = the type of bid, competitive or negotiated,

M = the maturity of the issue (for serial issues the average maturity),

L = the general level of interest rates.

The basic security for all general obligations is the tax guarantee of the issuing political unit. Hence I_g was not thought to be a function of the security offered to bondholders. While supplemental security, for example, utility revenues, may be offered on general obligations, not enough data were available to test for the effect, if any, of such supplemental security on the interest cost of issuing general obligations. Because virtually all general obligations must be offered at competitive bid, I_g was not considered to be a function of the type of bid. Too few general obligations were issued by state authorities to test adequately the significance of the type of issuer, state or state authority, on the interest cost of general obligations. So long as states guarantee bonds with full faith and credit taxing power, the instrumentality of issue, whether state or state authority, should have little effect on the interest cost of a general obligation issue. Hence I_g was not considered to depend upon the type of issuer.

The functions f and g were assumed to be linear and the parameters were estimated by multiple linear regression. To the extent that some of the relationships were nonlinear there is some loss in accuracy; however, the asset of simplicity was thought to outweigh any gains in accuracy that might have been achieved with a more complicated nonlinear approach.

In order to implement variables $T, R, P, S, C,$ and B, which are not subject to numerical measurement, the dummy variable approach was employed. This technique was also used to implement variable A, the amount of an issue, in order to avoid the biasing effect of extreme observations on the regression.

Relationships (1) and (2) can then be put in the following linear forms:

$$I_g = A + \sum_{i=0}^{2} B_{ri}X_{ri} + \sum_{i=0}^{2} B_{ai}X_{ai} + \sum_{i=0}^{3} B_{pi}X_{pi} + B_cX_c \qquad (3)$$
$$+ B_mX_m + B_LX_L$$

where

A = the constant term;

X_r = rating of issue—Aaa (X_{r0}), Aa (X_{r1}), A (X_{r2}). B_{r0} is set equal to zero to prevent perfect correlation;

X_a = amount of issue—over \$5 million (X_{a0}), \$1–5 million (X_{a1}), less than \$1 million (X_{a2}). B_{a0} is set equal to zero to prevent perfect correlation;

X_p = purpose of issue—all purposes other than roads, utilities, and education facilities (X_{p0}); roads (X_{p1}); utilities (X_{p2}); education facilities (X_{p3}). B_{p0} is set equal to zero to prevent perfect correlation;

X_c = 1 if callable, 0 if not callable;

X_m = average maturity in years;[6]

X_L = the long-term government bond yield at date of issue (an estimate of the general level of interest rates);

and

$$I_r = A + B_tX_t + \sum_{i=0}^{3} B_{ri}X_{ri} + \sum_{i=0}^{2} B_{ai}X_{ai} + \sum_{i=0}^{4} B_{pi}X_{pi}$$
$$+ \sum_{i=0}^{2} B_{si}X_{si} + B_cX_c + B_bX_b + B_mX_m + B_LX_L \qquad (4)$$

where

A = the constant term;

X_t = 1 if issued by state authority; 0 if issued by state;

X_r = rating of issue—Aaa or Aa (X_{r0}), A (X_{r1}), Baa (X_{r2}), unrated (X_{r3}). B_{r0} is set equal to zero to prevent perfect correlation (too few issues were rated Aaa to establish a separate category for that rating);

X_a = amount of issue—over \$5 million (X_{a0}), \$1–5 million (X_{a1}), less than \$1 million (X_{a2}). B_{a0} is set equal to zero to prevent perfect correlation;

X_p = purpose of issue—all purposes other than toll roads and bridges, nontoll roads and bridges, utilities, and education facilities (X_{p0}); toll roads and bridges (X_{p1}); nontoll roads and bridges (X_{p2}); utilities (X_{p3}); education facilities (X_{p4}). B_{p0} is set equal to zero to prevent perfect correlation;

X_s = security for issue—any security other than special tax revenues and state rental revenues (X_{s0}), special tax revenues (X_{s1}), state rental revenues (X_{s2}). B_{s0} is set equal to zero to prevent perfect correlation;

X_c = 1 if callable; 0 if not callable;

X_b = 1 if negotiated bid; 0 if competitive bid;

X_m = average maturity in years;

X_L = the long-term government bond yield at date of issue (an estimate of the general level of interest rates).

The matrix of simple correlation coefficients, the means, and the standard deviations of the variables in equations (3) and (4) are shown in Tables 32 and 33. Parameters of equations (3) and (4) estimated by multiple regression are shown in Tables 34 and 35. The B coefficients were accepted as significant if they were greater than $1\frac{1}{2}$ times their standard error. One great surprise appears among the results. The nature of a revenue bond as callable or not callable apparently has no significant effect on the interest cost. Although B_c in equation (4) is negative, as might be expected, the standard error is almost six times the size of the coefficient.

TABLE 32

Matrix of the simple correlation coefficients, means ($\overline{M}$), and standard deviations (s) of the variables in equation (3)

	X_{r1}	X_{r2}	X_{a1}	X_{a2}	X_{p1}	X_{p2}	X_{p3}	X_c	X_m	X_L	I_g	$\overline{M}$	s
X_{r1}	1.00	−.43	−.07	.15	−.15	.25	−.05	−.14	.09	−.06	.04	.59	.49
X_{r2}		1.00	.15	−.10	.12	−.11	−.03	−.12	−.01	−.12	.14	.11	.31
X_{a1}			1.00	−.31	−.18	.20	.01	.18	.06	−.05	−.04	.31	.46
X_{a2}				1.00	−.21	.20	−.04	.17	−.16	.06	.02	.18	.38
X_{p1}					1.00	−.18	−.23	.01	.03	.00	−.05	.16	.37
X_{p2}						1.00	−.22	.18	.38	−.08	.03	.14	.35
X_{p3}							1.00	−.05	−.08	.05	.03	.22	.41
X_c								1.00	−.26	.00	−.25	.75	.43
X_m									1.00	−.07	.30	12.36	4.52
X_L										1.00	.66	3.59	.42
I_g											1.00	3.08	.39

TABLE 33

Matrix of the simple correlation coefficients, means $(\overline{M})$, and standard deviations (s) of the variables in equation (4)

	X_t	X_{r1}	X_{r2}	X_{r3}	X_{g1}	X_{g2}	X_{p1}	X_{p2}	X_{p3}	X_{p4}	X_{s1}	X_{s2}	X_c	X_b	X_m	X_L	I_r	$\overline{M}$	s
X_t	1.00	−.08	.31	−.09	−.02	−.19	.27	.13	.25	−.54	−.23	.31	−.23	.20	.23	.01	.10	.34	.47
X_{r1}		1.00	−.20	−.59	−.02	−.03	−.02	.05	−.07	.09	.39	.06	−.36	−.03	−.13	−.02	−.13	.35	.48
X_{r2}			1.00	−.22	.26	−.13	−.04	.26	−.06	−.24	.16	−.04	.31	−.03	.02	.10	.09	.07	.25
X_{r3}				1.00	.04	−.22	−.09	−.43	−.09	.25	−.54	.00	.31	.20	.29	.09	.35	.40	.50
X_{g1}					1.00	−.46	−.19	.00	−.07	.01	.07	.00	−.03	.07	−.04	−.05	−.01	.35	.48
X_{g2}						1.00	−.25	−.24	−.04	.48	−.03	−.04	.12	−.05	−.21	−.01	−.01	.27	.45
X_{p1}							1.00	−.22	−.09	−.34	−.18	−.09	−.13	−.09	.31	.01	.16	.14	.34
X_{p2}								1.00	−.12	−.46	.41	.06	−.07	−.20	−.25	.12	−.15	.23	.42
X_{p3}									1.00	−.18	−.16	−.07	.01	.05	.17	.00	.12	.04	.21
X_{p4}										1.00	−.03	−.14	.15	−.08	−.06	−.01	.05	.42	.49
X_{s1}											1.00	−.24	−.15	−.23	−.34	−.06	−.22	.35	.48
X_{s2}												1.00	−.17	.11	−.07	.02	−.03	.10	.30
X_c													1.00	.06	−.11	.15	.27	.27	.44
X_b														1.00	.38	.33	.62	.21	.42
X_m															1.00		.81	14.94	9.34
X_L																1.00		3.51	.91
I_r																	1.00	3.37	.97

64

TABLE 34

Results of multiple regression, equation (3)

Independent variable	Coefficient of partial correlation of independent variable with dependent variable	B coefficients	Standard error of the B coefficients
X_{r1}	0.2374	0.1373	0.0367
X_{r2}	0.4067	0.3798	0.0558
X_{a1}	−0.0507	−0.0300	0.0558
X_{a2}	0.0488	0.0351	0.0470
X_{p1}	−0.0969	−0.0694	0.0466
X_{p2}	−0.0608	−0.0514	0.0551
X_{p3}	0.0129	0.0077	0.0390
X_c	−0.1086	−0.0724	0.0420
X_m	0.4365	0.0296	0.0040
X_L	0.7709	0.6798	0.0367

Constant term (A)	0.2246
Coefficient of determination (R^2)	0.6568
Coefficient of multiple correlation (R)	0.8104
Unexplained variance ($1-R^2$)	0.3431
Standard error of the estimate	0.2291
Standard deviation of I_g	0.3913
Sample size	245

TABLE 35

Results of multiple regression, equation (4)

Independent variable	Coefficient of partial correlation of independent variable with dependent variable	B coefficients	Standard error of the B coefficients
X_t	−0.0100	−0.0112	0.0770
X_{r1}	0.1554	0.1935	0.0850
X_{r2}	0.1885	0.3713	0.1337
X_{r3}	0.3698	0.5393	0.0940
X_{a1}	0.0883	0.0983	0.0767
X_{a2}	0.0839	0.1108	0.0910
X_{p1}	0.2307	0.3657	0.1066
X_{p2}	−0.0266	−0.0372	0.0966
X_{p3}	0.2058	0.4457	0.1466
X_{p4}	0.0681	0.0852	0.0864
X_{s1}	0.0656	0.0729	0.0767
X_{s2}	0.1508	0.2235	0.1013
X_c	−0.0131	−0.0127	0.0669
X_b	−0.0509	−0.0517	0.0701
X_m	0.4814	0.0311	0.0039
X_L	0.8503	0.7330	0.0314

Constant term (A)	0.1837
Coefficient of determination (R^2)	0.8567
Coefficient of multiple correlation (R)	0.9256
Unexplained variance ($1-R^2$)	0.1432
Standard error of the estimate	0.3664
Standard deviation of I_r	0.9681
Sample size	226

Another mild surprise is contained in the estimate of B_b in equation (4). While B_b is not significantly different from zero, it is negative, which implies that issuers secure more favorable rates at negotiated bid than at competitive bid. In view of the fact that the interest cost of issues sold at negotiated bid frequently covers the cost of aid and advice rendered by the underwriters, this result is somewhat surprising.

The other results might well have been anticipated. The amount of the issue, revenue bonds or general obligations, is not a significant determinant of the interest cost. From the results somewhat more confidence can be placed on this conclusion with respect to general obligations than with respect to revenue bonds.

The purpose of a general obligation issue is not a significant determinant of the interest cost. This coincides with the notion that the tax guarantee of the political unit is the basic consideration; what the political unit does with the funds is of little concern to investors, within some constraints, of course.

With no tax guarantee on revenue bonds, one might expect that the purpose of a revenue bond issue or the security offered to bondholders would affect the interest cost. The results indicate that funds borrowed for toll roads (and toll bridges) and utilities carry higher interest costs than funds borrowed for other purposes. The results also indicate that the interest cost of funds borrowed for nontoll roads (and bridges) and educational facilities is not significantly different from the interest cost of funds borrowed for purposes other than toll roads and utilities. Borrowed funds secured by rental revenues from the state cost more than borrowed funds secured by other revenue sources, special taxes, and public user charges.

The results show that the political status of the issuing unit, whether a public authority or the state itself, is not a significant determinant of the interest cost of borrowed funds. Apparently investors are not concerned with the political or corporate nature of the state instrumentality, provided, of course, that the instrumentality is clearly an arm of the state.

Assuming that B coefficients which are less than $1\frac{1}{2}$ times their standard error are not significantly different from zero, from equation (3):

$$B_{a1},\ B_{a2},\ B_{p1},\ B_{p2},\ B_{p3} = 0;$$

and from equation (4):

$$B_t,\ B_{a1},\ B_{a2},\ B_{p2},\ B_{p4},\ B_{s1},\ B_c,\ B_b = 0.$$

Rewriting equations (3) and (4) to exclude the variables which do not determine I_g and I_r and the variables whose coefficients were defined equal to zero:

$$I_g = A + B_{r1}X_{r1} + B_{r2}X_{r2} + B_cX_c + B_mX_m + B_LX_L, \qquad (5)$$

$$\begin{aligned} I_r = A &+ B_{r1}X_{r1} + B_{r2}X_{r2} + B_{r3}X_{r3} + B_{p1}X_{p1} \\ &+ B_{p3}X_{p3} + B_{s2}X_{s2} + B_mX_m + B_LX_L. \end{aligned} \qquad (6)$$

Estimates of the parameters of equations (5) and (6) were again obtained by multiple regression, and the results are shown in Tables 36 and 37. The estimated regression equations are as follows:

$$\begin{aligned} I_g = 0.2472 &+ 0.1363X_{r1} + 0.3613X_{r2} - 0.0929X_c + 0.0267X_m \\ &+ 0.6835X_L, \end{aligned} \qquad (7)$$

$$\begin{aligned} I_r = 0.3038 &+ 0.2833X_{r1} + 0.4237X_{r2} + 0.6215X_{r3} + 0.2709X_{p1} \\ &+ 0.3354X_{p3} + 0.1263X_{s2} + 0.0284X_m + 0.7272X_L. \end{aligned} \qquad (8)$$

TABLE 36

Results of multiple regression, equation (5)

Independent variable	Coefficient of partial correlation of independent variable with dependent variable	B coefficients	Standard error of the B coefficients
X_{r1}	0.2441	0.1363	0.0350
X_{r2}	0.3956	0.3613	0.0543
X_c	−0.1591	−0.0929	0.0373
X_m	0.4470	0.0267	0.0035
X_L	0.7705	0.6835	0.0366

Constant term (A)	0.2472
Coefficient of determination (R^2)	0.6491
Coefficient of multiple correlation (R)	0.8057
Unexplained variance ($1-R^2$)	0.3508
Standard error of the estimate	0.2318
Standard deviation of I_g	0.3913
Sample size	245

TABLE 37

Results of multiple regression, equation (6)

Independent variable	Coefficient of partial correlation of independent variable with dependent variable	B coefficients	Standard error of the B coefficients
X_{r1}	0.2522	0.2833	0.0738
X_{r2}	0.2448	0.4237	0.1139
X_{r3}	0.4907	0.6215	0.0749
X_{p1}	0.2198	0.2709	0.0816
X_{p3}	0.1754	0.3354	0.1278
X_{s2}	0.1005	0.1263	0.0848
X_m	0.5011	0.0248	0.0033
X_L	0.8540	0.7272	0.0301

Constant term (A)	0.3038
Coefficient of determination (R^2)	0.8510
Coefficient of multiple correlation (R)	0.9225
Unexplained variance ($1-R^2$)	0.1489
Standard error of the estimate	0.3736
Standard deviation of I_r	0.9681
Sample size	226

By selecting appropriate values for the variables in equations (7) and (8) and by combining the results in the form

$$I_a = I_r - I_g, \tag{9}$$

estimates of the added interest cost of issuing revenue bonds (I_a) under varying conditions can be obtained. Tables 20–23 in the text of this chapter were derived by plugging various values for the variables into equations (7) and (8) and combining the results in equation (9).

5

Other Costs Associated with Nonguaranteed Borrowing

ADDITIONAL INTEREST costs on borrowed funds are not the only cost of nonguaranteed financing of state projects in constitutionally limited states. In order for a restricted state to borrow without violating constitutional debt provisions, it must establish administrative procedures which satisfy the courts that such borrowing is not state debt. Typically, in the case of the public corporation, the administrative procedures may be circuitous in nature, thereby creating expenses for administering the debt over and above such expenses for administering full-faith and credit debt. Even where public corporations are not involved, the requirement that funds relating to revenue-financed projects be kept separate from general state funds may lead to added administrative costs.

Investors typically require the same insurance protection for revenue-financed projects that they require in private-enterprise investment. Self-insurance on the part of the state is generally not possible because of constitutional limitations, nor acceptable to investors in cases where states cannot directly guarantee the debt. As compared with full-faith and credit financing in which self-insurance is commonly used, the insurance costs of revenue projects are probably excessive.

Although not a necessary feature of nonguaranteed borrowing in constitutionally limited states, there appears to be a close relationship between debt limitations and the amount of state borrowing from state investment funds. Because the income from all state bonds is exempt from federal income taxes, the bonds

69

carry lower yields than other obligations of comparable risk. Inasmuch as all income of state investment funds is tax exempt, regardless where earned, state funds pay a premium for a tax exempt feature they cannot use when they purchase bonds of the state government. Then, too, state investment funds may be induced to finance revenue projects of their own state at rates lower than the state could otherwise obtain in the market. These two factors combine to understate the cost of state projects financed with own state funds, and the result is an inequitable use of retirement funds entrusted to states by their employees. To the extent that debt limitations lead to the practice of interagency lending of state funds, the loss of return on state funds and the inequities involved must be considered a cost of having a debt limitation.

Administrative Costs of Nonguaranteed Financing

The Council of State Governments found in its study of public authorities that corporations have a high degree of autonomy in such areas as budgeting, finance, and personnel. It is held in some circles that this autonomy, which insulates corporations from bureaucratic controls of government, enables government to perform functions of a revenue-producing nature with a high degree of efficiency.[1] Others have criticized this view on the grounds that calling the men a board of directors and the organization a corporation does not prove its efficiency.[2] Charles W. Ingler stated this position when he said:

and others believe that a public authority is likely to operate more efficiently than a governmental enterprise, in order to show a favorable balance sheet. However, a heavy burden of proof rests on the public authority in this connection. The authority is often subsidized by government, when government gives it a captive market; when government exempts its securities from taxation; and when government exempts it from public salary laws and permits it to raid key government personnel. It has been suggested that each state highway department should refuse to build any good free roads near to a turnpike except feeder roads. It is difficult to prove that a public authority, so heavily subsidized, is or is not efficient.

Some proponents of the public authority urge that the authority will benefit from its comparative freedom from customary routine controls of budget, personnel, and finance. It is a truism among public administrators, that when a governmental agency is set up in comparative isolation, with its own board, its own rotary fund, personnel classification systems—then everyone gets a raise and the rotary continuously builds up increasing balances. Because of this, many legislators and administrators hesitate to grant such exceptions. There is some question as to whether public authorities are wholly free of these disabilities, and if so, why?[3]

This conflict of opinion largely centers around the use of the public corporation in such areas as toll roads, port facilities, utilities, and other government functions in which user charges on the public generate authority revenues. A review of the literature does not reveal any definitive studies that resolve this conflict one way or the other; nor am I prepared to resolve the question in this study. It is not necessary for the demonstration of the thesis proposed herein. Nothing in the proposal to abandon state debt limitations denies states the right to use the corporate form of organization for the performance of state functions. Abandonment of debt limitations would merely free the state from the necessity of establishing special corporations whose sole *raison d'être* is to provide the administrative framework for constitutional circumvention and whose efficiency is doubtful.

There is no apparent conflict centering around the use of state corporations such as building authorities which were obviously created to circumvent debt limitations, and which have no other functions of a substantial nature. It seems to be generally held that such corporations are obnoxious devices created out of the contingencies of the moment. However, there do not appear to be any penetrating studies which have isolated and quantified the the inefficiencies of the corporate device as used solely for constitutional circumvention. The best that I could find was done by J. R. Rothermel, Jr., Secretary of the Wisconsin Building Commission.[4] From his experience with Wisconsin's building corporations, Rothermel has estimated the added administrative costs of debt financing by the corporate method in Wisconsin. He has broken down administrative costs into four areas: marketing costs, trustee's fees, loss of earnings on bond proceeds, and the general administrative expense.

In the marketing of bonds, Rothermel estimates an added cost of 0.03 per cent on $100 million of revenue financing via the corporate method. The added cost arises out of the more comprehensive fiscal advice required, bond counsel work, bond registration, and added printing expenses. He states:

The extra expense for fiscal advice is the result of the unique nature of our bond. We can't simply go into the market and sell them like a state will sell a general obligation. We've got to find out what part of the market can buy our securities, we have to scratch harder; tailor our issue more finely. And that takes added thinking and some pretesting of the market—that's what we pay for when we get fiscal advice from an investment banker or sell on a negotiated basis.

Because we are selling what is essentially a revenue bond we have to have an elaborate trust indenture, and extensive prospectus, and they have to be especially registered. We have the expenses of clearing this through the Securities Exchange Commission and the Internal Revenue Bureau each time; we have numerous copies of leases and subleases which have to be written; some 50 different documents that have to be prepared for our issue as against 12 for a general obligation of the State of Maryland. These items all produce extra cost.[5]

Rothermel estimates that trustee's fees exceed the cost of having a state paying agent by 0.015 per cent a year on a bond issue. This added expense arises out of the added services required of a trustee because of the nature of revenue bonds.

One of the major disadvantages of revenue bonds lies in the apparent difficulty in preparing draw-down features acceptable to investors. On general obligations it is simple to float portions of large bond issues as the funds are required. With revenue bonds, problems of investor security usually require that the entire issue be floated at once. The proceeds may then be reinvested until required, but generally at lower rates than the state agency or corporation pays on the bond issue. Also, the proceeds of each bond issue of a public corporation must be kept in a separate construction account and invested apart from the proceeds of other bond issues. This feature results in some inefficiency and consequent loss of return. Rothermel estimates this loss to be 0.03 per cent a year on a 17-year bond issue.

As to general administration of the corporation and its bond issues, Rothermel estimates added expenses of about 0.05 per cent a year for $50 million of bonds outstanding. The added expenses go to pay personnel that would not be needed if the bonds were administered directly by the state, and for materials which he estimates would not be required with general obligations.

The total of the added marketing costs, trustee's fees, loss of earnings, and added administrative expense is then estimated by Rothermel at 0.125 per cent. It should be noted here that these estimates apply only to the corporate device as established solely to administer the borrowing of funds for state projects, and not to public corporations which provide other public services such as the operation of toll roads or power facilities.

Added Insurance Costs

The cost of casualty insurance is probably greater for revenue financed projects than for full-faith and credit undertakings of a state for the following two reasons:

1. State authorities carry much more extensive insurance coverage, both as to amount and type, than state agencies normally carry.[6] Authority projects are generally 100 per cent bond financed. If the projects are financed by revenue bonds, bondholders have no legal recourse against states in the event of project failure, whether brought about by an insurable act of God or by unexpectedly low revenues. Because of little or no capital cushion and lack of legal recourse against states, revenue bondholders have typically required authorities to carry more insurance than would be required with full-faith and credit financing.

2. For the most part, authority insurance is carried with private casualty companies. In restricted states, debt limitations normally preclude insuring authority projects with state insurance funds, and few authorities are of sufficient size and diversity to use a bondholder-approved self-insurance program. Privately placed casualty insurance is likely to be more expensive than comparable state self-insurance if state resources are sufficient to permit a program of self-insurance.

A thorough study of these relationships is not possible here. They would be properly treated in a separate study by experts in the area of insurance. The function of this section is merely to indicate the added insurance costs that might exist and to attempt some rudimentary quantification.

TABLE 38

Insurance practices of state authorities

Type of insurance	Number of replies	Number carrying insurance	Number required by bond indenture	Number insuring with state fund
Fire and extended coverage	48	46	34	8
Public liability	48	40	27	2
Group health	48	25	0	0
Group hospital	48	20	0	0
Surety bond on employees	48	32	13	0
Performance bond from contractors	48	33	16	0
Other[a]	48	19	17	0

[a] Burglary, boiler, bridge property damage, marine, use and occupancy, etc.
Note: Constructed from my own survey of state authorities.

I surveyed state authorities as to types of insurance carried, insurance required by bondholders, use of state insurance funds, and recent premium and claims experience. The results of the survey relating to insurance practices, as shown in Table 38, indicate a rather widespread use of the various insurance types by state authorities. In its 1953 survey of public authorities the Council of State Governments obtained the following results: of 35 replying authorities, 35 carried fire insurance, 32 public liability, 10 group hospital, 7 group health, 32 surety bonds on employees, 32 contractors faithful performance, and 17 some other forms of insurance.[7] These results show a more widespread use of insurance by authorities than my survey shows.

Just how much less insurance would have been required on comparable undertakings financed by general obligations is difficult to predict. Some states have no formal self-insurance program, but meet any casualty losses with regular state appropriations. Other states have constructed insurance reserves along actuarial principles, but it is doubtful that formal self-insurance in those states is designed to cover all the contingencies covered by privately placed authority insurance. Other states have blanket insurance coverage with private companies, but again it is doubtful if the blanket coverage takes in as many contingencies as revenue bondholders would require.

Because of the actuarial problems involved, it is difficult to predict the added cost of private insurance carried by state authorities over the cost of comparable state self-insurance. In Wisconsin the State Insurance Fund has built an actuarial reserve against fire damage to state buildings by charging rates equal to one half the rates established by the Association of Fire Underwriters. This rate is apparently sufficient, because in 1955 the state legislature appropriated $5 million of the insurance fund's reserve into the general fund. This apparently could be done because of a favorable experience in fire damage to state property, because of smaller loading than private companies have, and because of whatever tax advantage state funds have. The State Insurance Fund in Wisconsin has seven full-time employees handling insurance of $327 million on state property representing 90 per cent of the estimated real value, plus a voluntary program for insuring the property of political subdivisions.

The results of my survey relating to the premiums and claims experience of state authorities are shown in Table 39. Because of the very principles of insurance, one could obviously not conclude that the difference between the premiums and claims represents the added cost of private insurance over a program of state self-insurance. A holocaust might occur tomorrow which would make the claims exceed the premiums. The results shown here, however, combined with other observations, lend credulity to the view that experience on state property is more favorable than on comparable private property from which rate making information is largely extracted.

Most states have sufficient resources to carry out programs of self-insurance on state projects. To the extent that this cannot

TABLE 39

Premiums and claims experience of seventeen state authorities, 1950–1959

Type of insurance	Total premiums paid	Total claims collected	Number of years experience	Number of years claims exceeded premiums
Fire and extended coverage	$4,976,065	$187,754	105	2
Other insurance (exclusive of health and hospital)	4,546,971	479,755	96	1
Total	$9,523,036	$667,509	201	3

Note: Constructed from my own survey of state authorities.

be done on projects financed by revenue bonds, and to the extent that private insurance is more costly, state debt limitations which compel revenue financing impose an additional insurance cost on state projects.

The Costs of Interagency Lending

In some states revenue projects have been financed by direct loans from state investment funds. This practice permits state authorities and agencies to obtain capital funds at lower rates than would otherwise be paid in the private capital market at the cost of a subnormal return on the investment of state funds. Ostensibly, the directors of state investment funds would not be required to make loans of this nature if the return were less than on comparable alternative investments. However, if the state legislature "authorizes" a state investment fund to lend money to a state authority or agency at low rates of interest, the fund's interest may well be subverted regardless of the directors' intentions. Such was the case with the construction of a $7,500,000 state office building in one state. The legislature authorized a state authority to issue bonds in that amount at 1.00 per cent interest, and at the same time authorized the state investment fund to finance the project by purchasing the bonds at par. No investigation is necessary to know that 1.00 per cent was significantly below the normal market return on that kind of investment. The state's interest cost on the project would be stated at 1.00 per cent of the value of the bond issue but, clearly, the real cost to the state is much higher when the loss of return to the state fund is taken into account. About this practice *Business Week* said the following:

Another questionable practice is using pension funds to help cities and towns [and state agencies] market their bonds at low interest rates. The aim of the town or city [or state agency] is directly counter to the goals of the fund trustees which is to get maximum yield. Often in such cases political pressure is brought to bear on fund officials. In Virginia, the Virginia Retirement System has bought state dormitory bonds [limited to 4.00 per cent] which the state had difficulty marketing.[8]

Business Week cited the case of the New York City Pension Fund of which 75 per cent of the assets are invested in city bonds. In 1959 they bought $264 million in city bonds at yields ranging from 3.00 per cent to 3.50 per cent, whereas they could have purchased Aaa public utilities yielding from 4.20 per cent to 4.70 per cent or even United States government bonds yielding from 3.60 per cent to 4.50 per cent. *Business Week* notes further: "A difference of 1 per cent in yield could mean several million dollars in additional earning for the fund. . . ."[9]

State legislatures need not enter the picture if proper administrative pressure is brought to bear on fund officials. In New York the State Comptroller is responsible for the investment of state funds and various fiduciary and trust funds under his control. At the same time, as chief financial officer of the state, he has "a sympathetic interest in the financial success and stability of State agencies including public authorities."[10] In such a dual position the Comptroller could well subvert the interest of state investment funds by making direct loans to New York State agencies or authorities at submarket rates of interest. In fact, the New York State Comptroller has purchased directly for state funds the bonds of the New York Dormitory Authority, the Industrial Exhibit Authority, the Whiteface Mountain Authority, and "others whose bonds were of dubious marketability."[11] In its report on public authorities in New York, the Temporary Commission on Coordination of State Activities in New York State recommends that authorities be forbidden to make direct sales of bonds to funds controlled by the State Comptroller. It further recommends that any purchase of bonds of state authorities or agencies by state funds be made at public sale in competition with private capital.[12] The Temporary Commission goes on to say that this recommendation would "prevent this situation."[13]

One could legitimately wonder whether such a law would prevent situations where state funds are invested in own state projects at low interest rates. If there were a genuine desire on the part of New York State officials to finance state revenue projects at low rates by use of state funds, some method of circumventing such a law would surely be devised. Could not a separate corporation be established to purchase authority bonds at low interest rates and in turn resell the bonds to one of the state funds? If the resale could be construed to be a public sale, such action would be legal. One could not predict how New York courts would react to this situation; however, as a general rule, legal restrictions of this nature are easily circumvented if a genuine desire exists on the part of state officials.

At the heart of the problem lies the existence of constitutional debt restrictions in New York and other states where the same situation exists. If general obligations could be issued, there would be little reason to secure lower rates through state funds. States would clearly be better off to float the general obligations in the private market and invest state funds in some other type of security. Without debt restrictions states could issue revenue bonds if they genuinely wished to shift the risk of project failure to private investors. In this case there would be no reason for state funds to purchase the revenue bonds, because that action would deny the very reason for issuing revenue bonds in the first place, the shifting of the risk. Only with constitutional debt limitations is there an argument for the investment of state funds in state revenue projects. In the latter case, directors of state funds can know what debt restrictions prevent private investors from knowing, namely, that revenue bonds are virtually safe because the state intends paying off whether the project succeeds or fails.

One might argue that this knowledge of the risk imputes an advantage to the use of state funds in own state projects. To the extent that interest rates were arrived at by bargaining in light of the risk factor and other factors involved, this argument seems substantially correct. However, the state fund is still paying for the unnecessary tax-exempt feature of state bonds. Normally, bonds of the federal government to which perfect safety can be imputed carry higher yields than state bonds, because the income from federal bonds is not tax exempt to individuals. It seems clear that fund contributors would be better off if the funds were invested in federal government bonds at 4.0 per cent rather than own state bonds at 3.5 per cent. In essence, states forego the opportunity of trading on the tax-exempt feature of state bonds when they use their own funds to finance state projects.

If the foregoing analyses are substantially correct, one would expect that only in states with constitutional restrictions against

TABLE 40

Holdings of own state securities by state investment funds in 1958
(thousands of dollars)

Absolutely restricted states	Holdings of own state securities	Referendum states	Holdings of own state securities	Unrestricted states	Holdings of own state securities
Ariz.	$ 2,494	Ark.	$ 4,376	Conn.	$ 500
Colo.	1,750	Calif.	33,115	Mass.	5
Fla.	10,464	Idaho	2,940	Miss.	92
Ga.	10,006	Ill.	1,000	Tenn.	53
Ind.	2,200	Ky.	1,601		
La.	46,658	N.J.	19,814	Subtotal	$ 650
Mich.	1,764	N.Y.	113,862		
Minn.	5,800	R.I.	470	Md.	7,307
Nev.	1,260	S.C.	21,451		
Pa.	90,979	Va.	15,688		
Tex.	825	Wash.	29,967		
W.Va.	4,770				
Wis.	2,108				
Total	$181,078		$244,284		$7,957

Source: Bureau of the Census, *Compendium of State Government Finances*, 1958.

debt would state funds be invested significantly in the bonds of authorities or agencies of the same state. Results taken from the Bureau of the Census data confirm this observation, as shown in Table 40. With the exception of Maryland, investment of state funds in own state projects is almost nil in the unrestricted states; and Maryland has a deceptively forceful debt restriction, as shown in Chapter 3. On the other hand, states which must submit debt proposals to referendum had more than $244 million invested in own state projects in 1958; and absolutely restricted states had more than $181 million invested in own state projects in the same year.

In order to determine the nature of investment fund holdings of own state debt, I surveyed twenty-three investment funds in seventeen states which have significantly followed the practice of interagency lending. Of the twenty-one funds replying that they held bonds of own state agencies, seventeen reported holding only revenue bonds, one reported holding only general obligations, and three reported holding both types of obligations. From the results of the survey it seems clear that the bulk of the own state security holdings of state investment funds are revenue bonds.

When asked whether they had been directed by the state legislature to purchase state bonds, only one state fund replied "yes," but the qualified answer on other questionnaires indicated that the question was asked improperly. A few funds reported that they had been "authorized" to purchase bonds, and they indicated that this permissive authority was actually a directive. Had the question been framed in terms of "authorization," probably many more "yes" replies would have been given; however, in this case one could not be sure of the significance of the responses.

The survey showed that ten funds acquired the securities directly from the issuing agency, five funds purchased them on the open market, and six funds acquired state securities by both methods. To the extent that state bonds were purchased on the open market, it might imply that officials of the purchasing fund considered the securities wise investments. After the bonds had been sold in the market, the state fund could not subsequently lower the borrowing cost to the issuing agency by its purchase of the bonds. In two instances, however, state funds replied by saying they had been the sole bidder from the underwriters in the open market purchases.

Of the sixteen state investment funds acquiring securities directly from the issuing agency, twelve reported that the interest rate was set by negotiation between the fund and the issuing agency; four reported that the legislature or some administrative body had set the interest rate. The option of negotiating the rate implies that the state funds had some discretion in their purchase of the state bonds, but how much is questionable.

To the extent that state agencies and authorities sell their bonds to state investment funds at subnormal rates of interest, the interest cost of state projects will be understated. Any calculation of the real interest cost on projects thus financed must make allowance for the loss of income to state investment funds. Furthermore, the practice of interagency lending may result in an inequitable use of retirement funds contributed by state employees. The bulk of the funds available to states for investment comes from state employee or teacher retirement programs. Fund contributors have a vested interest in making the greatest possible return consistent with investment safety. To the extent that interagency lending offers a lower return to retirement funds than could otherwise be obtained on investments of comparable risk, the interests of fund contributors are violated whenever state funds invest in own state projects.

As long as constitutional restrictions plague state debt programs it seems likely that the practice of interagency lending of state funds will continue. If states repealed constitutional debt restrictions, interagency lending would in all likelihood disappear as a major instrument of state debt finance.

6

Conclusions and Policy Implications

I N VIEW of the discussion in the previous chapters, it seems clear that most states would do well to consider the revision of debt provisions in their constitutions. The decisions of state courts have so altered the impact of constitutional restrictions on state debt that these restrictions give little more than lip service to the limitation of borrowing activities of state legislatures. The possible policy implications of this study are many, but prior to a discussion of policies let us review the salient points made in the previous chapters.

Summary of the Findings

After the unfavorable debt experience of states during the depression of 1837, they adopted constitutional restrictions against borrowing. Caught up in the frontier movement, many states overextended themselves trying to capitalize on transportation innovations of the period: canals, railroads, and turnpikes. Declining enterprise revenues failed to support top-heavy debt structures and nine states defaulted on their obligations, four of which eventually repudiated part of their debt. In many states a disillusioned electorate forced the adoption of constitutional amendments limiting legislative power to incur debt and set the pattern of constitutional development for states yet to enter the Union. Today, forty of forty-eight state constitutions (Hawaii and Alaska not included) prevent state legislatures from borrowing for public improvements. In twenty states improvement debt may be incurred after a referendum, but in the other twenty states borrowing for public improvements requires a constitutional amendment. Among the eight "free" states, three are somewhat limited by special legislative majority provisions or provisions which limit the term of the debt. Only five states have in no way inhibited the borrowing power of their legislatures.

Since 1900, states have whittled away the force of their debt limitations by developing methods of borrowing which escape constitutional restrictions. The salient characteristics of this development have been legislative trial and error and judicial interpretation. State legislatures proposed borrowing schemes designed to escape constitutional bans. If state courts upset the plans on constitutional grounds, the plans were revised until the courts gave way and sanctioned the borrowing. Out of this development have come revenue bonds, public authorities, lease-purchase agreements, and reimbursement obligations. Although the development process has not ended, most states now find themselves able to borrow for public improvements of any nature, constitutional restrictions notwithstanding. The impact of the development of nonguaranteed methods of borrowing can be noted in the changing structure of state debts. Fifty years ago nonguaranteed debt was almost nonexistent. Twenty years ago it amounted to less than 15 per cent of total state debt. Today, nonguaranteed debt accounts for more than 50 per cent of the outstanding state debt. Contrary to a widely held belief, one of the impacts of nonguaranteed borrowing has not been to increase the burden of state debt. On the basis of comparison of state debt with personal income, the burden of state debt has increased very little in the past thirty years. The main impact of nonguaranteed borrowing has been on the structure of state debt, not on the burden state debt places on the taxpaying public.

The findings of this study challenge the contention that constitutional provisions have effectively limited state debt. Although a raw comparison between groups of states with similar constitutional provisions seems to uphold this contention, a closer analysis casts doubt on its validity. When the variant relationships between states and political subdivisions are taken into account, much of the differential between the groups of states dissolves. When the interest costs of state debt as a measure of burden are compared, the differential between states dissolves even further. The least that can be said is that there is no apparent tendency for a runaway state debt to occur in states without constitutional restrictions against state debt. The state currently in the most difficulty—West Virginia because of her toll road—is a state with an absolute debt restriction.

The findings of this study further substantiate the belief that nonguaranteed borrowing carries significantly higher interest costs than borrowing for which a state's credit is pledged. On the basis of a weighted average interest cost for the two types of debt in all states, this differential was 0.56 per cent in 1957, 0.48 per cent in 1958, and 0.66 per cent in 1959. For individual states nonguaranteed borrowing can result in a substantial increase in the burden of interest costs. To the extent that states intend paying off their revenue bonds regardless of the outcome of projects for which the bonds were issued, but are prevented by debt restrictions from making this intention clear to investors, the additional interest cost on nonguaranteed borrowing represents a real cost to the issuing state.

Other costs arise out of the use of nonguaranteed borrowing procedures. In many cases the administrative organization required to put borrowing beyond constitutional bans is more costly than comparable administration of full-faith and credit financing. This is especially true for public corporations whose sole function is to borrow money under the corporate banner. States are generally precluded from using self-insurance practices on nonguaranteed projects, resulting in greater insurance costs. There seems to be a significant correlation between debt limitations and interagency lending of state funds. To the extent that restricted states engage in the practice of borrowing from state investment funds to finance nonguaranteed projects at lower rates than would be obtainable in the market, debt limitations result in an understatement of project costs and an inequitable use of funds entrusted to those states.

A Policy Proposal

In view of the above findings, I propose that full borrowing power be restored to state legislatures, with no referendum requirements, nor any other restriction currently found in state constitutions. This proposal would not give legislatures more power to incur excessive state debts than they already possess, but it would improve the options available to states in the planning of a sound debt policy.

A strong case could be made for the use of public debt to finance works of internal improvement; however, it is not the intent of this study to make such a case. The policy proposed above should not be regarded as a recommendation that states incur debts for public improvements. The policy merely recognizes that states do exhibit a desire to borrow and accepts this desire as neither good nor bad. While it might be difficult to believe that one who regarded public borrowing as undesirable would propose this policy, it would be perfectly plausible to do so. One must recognize the irrevocable fact that state legislatures, and presumably the electorate, desire to borrow for public improvements. Disagreeing with this desire does not alter the fact. A policy of no public borrowing can only be implemented in the political arena by electing public managers who subscribe to this policy. Once the election is lost, the public interest would be best served by giving public managers the widest possible choice among alternative methods of borrowing. Abolition of constitutional debt restrictions would serve this public interest.

This policy does not condemn the use of nonguaranteed borrowing techniques, but only the constitutional restrictions which force their use. Rational public managers must consider the use of borrowing techniques which shift the risk of enterprise failure to lenders of funds. The rational use of revenue bonds depends, however, on the freedom of public managers to weigh the alternative of pledging a state's credit. The selection of revenue bonds over general obligations should depend on the managers' estimate of the public's willingness to accept or reject risk, not on constitutional considerations which force selection of revenue bonds.

The proposed policy does not condemn the concept of the public authority as a useful tool of government. If other studies can demonstrate their efficiency as government instrumentalities, the policy proposed herein does not preclude their use. General obligation bonds as well as revenue bonds may be used in conjunction with the public corporation.[1] If constitutional debt limitations were repealed, however, selection of the public authority format would depend on its efficiency, not on its usefulness as a method of borrowing outside state constitutions.

Some Criticisms and Counterproposals

In the literature and in my discussions with persons directly concerned in this matter, I have encountered numerous criticisms and counterproposals to the policy proposed above. Some have taken the position that state debt be restricted by some measure of a state's prosperity. For instance, the amount of permissible debt could be tied to personal income of state residents, assessed valuation of state property, average revenue of the state government, or any other reasonable measure of well being.[2] This policy would enable state legislatures to refund nonguaranteed debts into general obligations, thereby reaping some saving in interest expense and administrative expense. Simultaneously, such a constitutional provision would prevent states from incurring excessive debt.

Aside from difficulties in the application of such a constitutional provision, I believe such a proposal to be undesirable on several grounds. (1) There is no means of estimating reasonableness of future debt. As states grow wealthier, perhaps they will be able to afford relatively more debt, or perhaps relatively less debt. (2) If future legislatures desired to exceed the rate of borrowing permitted by constitutional provisions, present loopholes, or new loopholes if required, could be used to evade the limitation. (3) Such a provision would be extremely permissive in character. It seems likely that legislatures would regard such a provision as a mandate from the people to borrow up to the limit set in the constitution.[3] Rational debt management would be difficult under those circumstances.

Others have proposed that states generally adopt the referendum requirement now present in twenty state constitutions. Such action would permit the assumption of present nonguaranteed debt in those states where a pledge of the state's credit is now impossible without constitutional amendment. It would also permit future borrowing with general obligations, but keep the reins in the hands of the electorate, hopefully forestalling the possibility of a runaway state debt. While the proposal would improve the options available in some states, it would not change the position of states currently having referendum provisions in their constitutions. This latter group of states, as shown in Chapter 3, has relatively as large a debt as states currently unrestricted in borrowing matters. A referendum provision does not forestall rapid increases in state debt, because nonguaranteed borrowing is available without resort to a referendum. In Kentucky, a referendum state, the Legislative Research Commission had this to say:

> This constitutional arrangement for general obligation bonds [that is, the requirement of a referendum for deficits in excess of $500,000], designed as a directive and safeguard, has served as an effective deterrent. Administrative officials do not relish a statewide drive to gain acceptance of a debt proposal. However, through its corporate agencies the state has employed revenue bonds, which are exempt from the constitutional provisions.[4]

In other words, a referendum provision deters rapid increases in full-faith and credit debt because of the difficulty and cost of holding a referendum, but does not prevent excessive increases in total debt of which nonguaranteed debt is a part. If a state legislature wishes to borrow without troubling with a referendum, it is generally free to do so through one of the nonguaranteed methods. The cost of referendums and the legislative desire to avoid them should not be the deciding factors in the type of obligation selected for issuance by a state. The public should elect responsible officials. If it does not do so, a referendum requirement in a state constitution is not going to protect the public from improper management of state debt.

A third approach to the debt problem calls for the restoration of borrowing power to state legislatures with the requirement that a special legislative majority support any act of borrowing. This rule is currently followed in Massachusetts and Delaware. It is clear that this approach would increase the options available to state legislatures. When large majorities in the legislature favored debt proposals, the borrowing could be accomplished with general obligations or revenue bonds as the majority would desire. The problem arises in the gray area where a majority of legislators smaller than the required special majority favors a debt proposal. If the proponents of the borrowing act so desired they could bypass the constitutional requirement by use of revenue bonds.

Whether the majority would in fact bow to the will of the constitution or use revenue bonds in this gray area is difficult to predict. In 1957 the per capita state debts in Delaware and Massachusetts were $350 and $209 respectively, ranking one and two in the nation. This compares with per capita debts of $172 in Connecticut, $39 in Mississippi, $91 in New Hampshire, $31 in Tennessee, and $42 in Vermont, the five completely unrestricted states. When local debt is included, Delaware falls to second rank behind New York, and Massachusetts falls to sixth behind Maryland, Connecticut, and Washington. Although these data do not prove that the special majority requirements in Massachusetts and Delaware have not limited the amount of state debt, it seems clear that this constitutional provision has not significantly deterred the borrowing activities of those states.

A fourth approach, reflecting an adamant opposition to any state borrowing, proposes that present nonguaranteed debts be refunded into general obligations, and further that constitutional restrictions against future debt be made more complete, thereby closing the loopholes that currently exist. Their general philosophy could be stated thus: "Mistakes were made in state finance. Let us rectify, as much as possible, these mistakes by outrightly assuming nonguaranteed obligations; and then prevent future mistakes by closing constitutional loopholes which made the mistakes possible."

I believe such a policy to be undesirable, or at least unworkable, on several grounds. (1) State legislatures would be unlikely to close the very loopholes they are currently using. (2) Even if the present legislature and electorate could be so influenced, there is no guarantee that future legislatures will obey. When future legislatures wish to borrow, it seems likely that they will discover new loopholes in any provision that could be made part of state constitutions. Writing a law without loopholes is a difficult, if not an impossible, task. At such time as future legislatures developed methods of avoiding the newly adopted provisions, states would be in exactly the same position they are now. (3) It is not very clear that states have made mistakes by borrowing funds for public improvements. Certainly, no such assumption should be made without greater study of this controversial question.

A fifth group seems to be content with the present situation.[5] This group believes that states occasionally must borrow, and nonguaranteed methods and referendums make that possible; but constitutional restrictions provide a sufficient obstacle to widespread borrowing. The main prop to this argument has been the observation that debt in restricted states tends to be less than in unrestricted states. On the basis of the analysis in Chapter 3, this observation seems of doubtful validity. Even if the observation is granted, it seems likely, with continuing development of nonguaranteed methods of borrowing in the restricted states, that the force of constitutional restrictions as obstacles against state borrowing will eventually wither away.

The basic criticism of these five alternative proposals is that they involve relocation or change in the nature of barriers against state borrowing. Why establish barriers at all when the means of penetration are available? All of these proposals reflect the fear that state legislatures will resort to the "easy" method of financing public projects—borrowing—if they are given half a chance. However, because of nonguaranteed methods, they already have the opportunity of using the "easy" method. It is granted that states with full borrowing freedom might incur excessive debt. Some states have in the past. However, nonguaranteed methods afford equal opportunity for restricted states to maneuver themselves into a similarly overextended debt position. Under these circumstances it would seem that the best approach to the problem is the removal of barriers against state borrowing which merely restrict the form of the debt and not the amount or the purpose of the debt.

Some Practical Politics

I have been informed that, whatever the merits of my proposal, practical politics preclude its immediate adoption. While the electorate might be induced to move in the direction of more freedom for state legislatures to borrow funds, it is unlikely that this big a step could be taken all at once.

If this is truly the case, then one must bow to the irrepressible force of politics and accept some compromise that is close to his position. The proposal of free borrowing power subject to special legislative majority would be a big step in the right direction. At least some discretion would be afforded state legislatures in the selection of borrowing methods. If this is too much for the electorate to accept, then the next acceptable alternative is the restoration of legislative borrowing power subject to limitation by some measure of state prosperity. For the twenty absolutely restricted states the adoption of referendum provisions would increase the options available to the state legislatures in borrowing matters.

To move in the direction of stronger debt restrictions would be inappropriate. While state legislatures might be temporarily stymied, it probably would not be long before new borrowing techniques were devised if the legislatures evinced a true desire to borrow. In the absence of this desire, borrowing restrictions are not needed in any event.

REFERENCE MATTER

Appendix A

TEXTS OF STATE CONSTITUTIONAL DEBT PROVISIONS*

ALABAMA (1901)

"After the ratification of this constitution, no new debt shall be created against, or incurred by the state, or its authority except to repel invasion or suppress insurrection, and then only by a concurrence of two-thirds of the members of each house of the legislature, and the vote shall be taken by yeas and nays and entered on the journals; provided, the governor may be authorized to negotiate temporary loans, never to exceed three hundred thousand dollars, to meet the deficiencies in the treasury, and until the same is paid no new loan shall be negotiated; (provided, further, that this section shall not be so construed as to prevent the issuance of bonds for the purpose of refunding the existing bonded indebtedness of the state . . .). Any act creating or incurring any new debt against the state, except as herein provided for, shall be absolutely void . . . . " (Amendment XXVI, Article XXIII, Section 213, ratified 1933.)

ALASKA (1958)

"No state debt shall be contracted unless authorized by law for capital improvements and ratified by a majority of the qualified voters of the State who vote on the question. The State may, as provided by law and without ratification, contract debt for the purpose of repelling invasion, suppressing insurrection, defending the State in war, meeting natural disasters, or redeeming indebtedness outstanding at the time this constitution becomes effective." (Article IX, Section 8.)

ARIZONA (1912)

"The State may contract debts to supply the casual deficits or failures in revenues, or to meet expenses not otherwise provided for; but the aggregate amount of such debts, direct and contingent, whether

* With the exception of Alaska and Hawaii the following excerpts from state constitutions were taken from The Tax Foundation, *Constitutional Debt Control in the States,* Appendix I. Excerpts for Alaska and Hawaii were taken directly from their constitutions.

contracted by virtue of one or more laws, or at different periods of time, shall never exceed the sum of three hundred and fifty thousand dollars; and the money arising from the creation of such debts shall be applied to the purpose for which it was obtained or to repay the debts so contracted, and to no other purpose.

"In addition to the above limited power to contract debts the State may borrow money to repel invasion, suppress insurrection, or defend the State in time of war; but the money thus raised shall be applied exclusively to the object for which the loan shall have been authorized or to the payment of the debt thereby created . . . . " (Article IX, Section 5.)

"Questions upon bond issues or special assessments shall be submitted to the vote of real property taxpayers, who shall also in all respects be qualified electors of this State, and of the political subdivisions thereof affected by such question." (Article VII, Section 13, Amendment effective 1930.)

ARKANSAS (1874)

"Neither the State nor any city, county, town or other municipality in this State, shall ever lend its credit for any purpose whatever; . . . and the State shall never issue any interest-bearing treasury warrants or scrip." (Amendment No. 13, 1926.)

"Except for the purpose of refunding the existing outstanding indebtedness of the State and for assuming and refunding valid outstanding road improvement district bonds, the State of Arkansas shall issue no bonds or other evidence of indebtedness pledging the faith and credit of the State or any of its revenues for any purpose whatsoever, except by and with the consent of the majority of the qualified electors of the State voting on the question at a general election or at a special election called for that purpose." (Amendment No. 20, declared adopted 1935.)

CALIFORNIA (1879)

"The Legislature shall not, in any manner create any debt or debts, liability or liabilities, which shall, singly or in the aggregate with any previous debts or liabilities, exceed the sum of $300,000, except in case of war to repel invasion or suppress insurrection, unless the same shall be authorized by law for some single object or work to be distinctly specified therein which law shall provide ways and means, exclusive of loans, for the payment of the interest of such debt or liability as it falls due, and also to pay and discharge the principal of such debt or liability within 75 years of the time of the contracting thereof, and shall be irrepealable until the principal and interest thereon shall be paid and discharged, and such law may make provision for a sinking fund to pay the principal of such debt or liability to commence at a time after the incurring of such debt or liability of not more than a period of one-fourth of the time of maturity of such debt or liability; but no such law shall take effect until, at a general election, it shall have been submitted to the people and shall have received a majority of all the votes cast for and against it at such election; and all moneys raised by authority of such law shall be applied only to the specific object therein stated or to the payment of the debt thereby created, and such law shall be published in at least one newspaper in each county, or city and county, if one be published therein throughout the State for three months next preceding the election at which it is submitted to the people. The Legislature may, at any time after the approval of such law by the people, if no debt shall have been contracted in pursuance thereof, repeal the same." (Article XVI, Section 1, Amendment adopted 1908.)

Colorado (1876)

"The state shall not contract any debt by loan in any form, except to provide for casual deficiencies of revenue, erect public buildings for the use of the state, suppress insurrection, defend the state, or, in time of war, assist in defending the United States; and the amount of debt contracted in any one year to provide for deficiencies of revenue, shall not exceed one-fourth of a mill on each dollar of valuation of taxable property within the state, and the aggregate amount of such debt shall not any time exceed three-fourths of a mill on each dollar of said valuation, until the valuation shall equal one hundred millions of dollars, and thereafter such debt shall not exceed one hundred thousand dollars; and the debt incurred in any one year for erection of public buildings shall not exceed one-half mill on each dollar of said valuation; and the aggregate amount of such debt shall never at any time exceed the sum of fifty thousand dollars (except as [elsewhere] . . . provided), and in all cases the valuation in this section mentioned shall be that of the assessment last preceding the creation of said debt:" (Article XI, Section 3, Amendments adopted 1910 and 1920.)

"In no case shall any debt above mentioned in this article be created except by a law which shall be irrepealable, until the indebtedness therein provided for shall have been fully paid or discharged; such law shall specify the purpose to which the funds so raised shall be applied, and provide for the levy of a tax sufficient to pay the interest on and extinguish the principal of such debt within the time limited by such law for the payment thereof, which in the case of debts contracted for the erection of public buildings and supplying deficiencies of revenue shall not be less than ten nor more than fifteen years, and the funds arising from the collection of any such tax shall not be applied to any other purpose than that provided in the law levying the same, and when the debt thereby created shall be paid or discharged, such tax shall cease and the balance, if any, to the credit of the fund shall immediately be placed to the credit of the general fund of the state." (Article XI, Section 4.)

DELAWARE (1897)

"No money shall be borrowed or debt created by or on behalf of the State but pursuant to an Act of the General Assembly, passed with the concurrence of three-fourths of all the members elected to each House, except to supply casual deficiencies of revenue, repel invasion, suppress insurrection, defend the State in war, or pay existing debts; and any law authorizing the borrowing of money by or on behalf of the State shall specify the purpose for which the money is to be borrowed, and the money so borrowed shall be used exclusively for such purpose; but should the money so borrowed or any part thereof be left after the abandonment of such purpose, or the accomplishment thereof, such money, or the surplus thereof, may be disposed of according to law." (Article VIII, Section 3.)

FLORIDA (1887)

"The Legislature shall have power to provide for issuing State bonds only for the purpose of repelling invasion or suppressing insurrection. . . . " (Article IX, Section 6.)

GEORGIA (1945)

"No debt shall be contracted by, or on behalf of, the State, except to supply such temporary deficit as may exist in the treasury in any year for necessary delay in collecting the taxes of that year, to repel invasion, suppress insurrection and defend the State in time of war, or to pay the existing public debt; but the debt created to supply deficiencies in revenue shall not exceed, in the aggregate, five hundred thousand dollars, and any loan made for this purpose shall be repaid out of the taxes levied for the year in which the loan is made. However, said debt may be increased in the sum of three million, five hundred thousand dollars for the payment of the public school teachers of the State only. The principal amount borrowed for payment of teachers shall be repaid each year out of the common school appropriation, and the interest paid thereon shall be paid each year out of the general funds of the State.

"The bonded debt of the State shall never be increased, except to repel invasion, suppress insurrection or defend the State in time of war.

"All laws authorizing the borrowing of money by or on behalf of the State shall specify the purpose for which the money is to be used and the money so obtained shall be used for the purpose specified and for no other." (Article VII, Section III, Paragraphs I-III.)

"The General Assembly shall raise by taxation each year, in addition to the sum required to pay the public expenses, such amounts as are necessary to pay the interest on the public debt and the principal of the public debt maturing in such year and to provide a sinking fund to pay off and retire the bonds of the State which have not then matured. The amount of such annual levy shall be determined after consideration of the amount then held in the sinking fund. The taxes levied for such purposes and the said sinking fund, shall be applied to no other purpose whatever . . . . " (Article VII, Section III, Paragraph IX.)

HAWAII (1959)

"All bonds and other instruments of indebtedness issued by or on behalf of the State . . . must be authorized by the legislature . . . .

"Sixty million dollars is established as the limit of the funded debt of the State at any time outstanding and unpaid. Bonds and other instruments of indebtedness in excess of such limit may be issued when authorized by a two-thirds vote of all the members to which each house of the legislature is entitled, provided such excess debt, at the time of authorization, would not cause the total of state indebtedness to exceed a sum equal to fifteen per cent of the total assessed values for tax rate purposes of real property in the State . . . .

"Instruments of indebtedness to meet appropriations for any fiscal period in anticipation of the collection of revenues for such period or to meet casual deficits or failures of revenue, which shall be payable within one year, and bonds or other instruments of indebtedness to suppress insurrection, to repel invasion, to defend the State in war or to meet emergencies caused by disaster or other act of God, may be issued by the State under legislative authorization without regard to any debt limit.

"All bonds or other instruments of indebtedness for a term exceeding one year shall be in serial form maturing in substantially equal annual installments, the first installment to mature not later than five years from the date of the issue of such series, and the last installment not later than thirty-five years from the date of such issue. Interest and principal payments shall be a first charge on the general revenues of the State . . . .

"The provisions of this section shall not be applicable to indebtedness incurred under revenue bond statutes by a public enterprise of the state . . . or public corporation, when the only security for such indebtedness is the revenues of such enterprise or public corporation . . . .

"Nothing in this section shall prevent the refunding of any indebtedness at any time." (Article VI, Section 3.)

IDAHO (1890)

"The legislature shall not in any manner create any debt or debts, liability or liabilities, which shall singly or in the aggregate, exclusive of the debt of the territory at the date of its admission as a state, and exclusive of debts or liabilities incurred subsequent to January 1, 1911, for the purpose of completing the construction and furnishing of the state capitol at Boise, Idaho, and exclusive of debt or debts, liability or liabilities incurred by the eleventh session of the legislature of the state of Idaho, exceed in the aggregate the sum of two million dollars, except in case of war, to repel an invasion, or suppress an insurrection, unless the same shall be authorized by law, for some single object or work, to be distinctly specified therein, which law shall provide ways and means, exclusive of loans, for the payment of the interest on such debt or liability as it falls due, and also for the payment and discharge of the principal of such debt or liability within twenty years of the time of the contracting thereof, and shall be irrepealable until the principal and interest thereon shall be paid and discharged. But no such law shall take effect until at a general election it shall have been submitted to the people, and shall have received a majority of all the votes cast for or against it at such election, and all moneys raised by the authority of such laws shall be applied only to specified objects therein stated or to the payment of the debt thereby created, and such law shall be published in at least one newspaper in each county, or city and county, if one be published therein, throughout the state for three months next preceding the election at which it is submitted to the people. The legislature may at any time after the approval of such law, by the people, if no debts shall have been contracted in pursuance thereof, repeal the same." (Article VIII, Section 1.)

ILLINOIS (1870)

" . . . the state may to meet casual deficits or failures in revenues, contract debts, never to exceed in the aggregate $250,000; and moneys thus borrowed shall be applied to the purpose for which they were obtained, or to pay the debt thus created, and to no other purpose; and no other debt, except for the purpose of repelling invasion, suppressing insurrection, or defending the state in war (for payment of which the faith of the state shall be pledged), shall be contracted, unless the law authorizing the same shall, at a general election, have been submitted to the people, and have received a majority of the votes cast for members of the general assembly at such election . . . and provision shall be made, at the time, for the payment of the interest annually, as it shall accrue, by a tax levied for the purpose or from other sources of revenue; which law, providing for the payment of such interest by such tax, shall be irrepealable until such debt be paid: And, provided, further, that the law levying the tax shall be submitted to the people with the law authorizing the debt to be contracted." (Article IV, Section 18.)

INDIANA (1851)

"No law shall authorize any debt to be contracted, on behalf of the State, except in the following cases: To meet casual deficits in the revenue; to pay the interest on the State debt; to repel invasion, suppress insurrection, or, if hostilities be threatened, provide for the public defense." (Article 10, Section 5.)

IOWA (1857)

"The State may contract debts to supply casual deficits or failures in revenues, or to meet expenses not otherwise provided for; but the aggregate amount of such debts, direct and contingent, whether contracted by virtue of one or more acts of the General Assembly, or at different periods of time, shall never exceed the sum of two hundred and fifty thousand dollars; and the money arising from the creation of such debts, shall be applied to the purpose for which it was obtained, or to repay the debts so contracted, and to no other purpose whatever." (Article VII, Section 2.)

"In addition to the above limited power to contract debts, the State may contract debts to repel invasion, suppress insurrection, or defend the State in war; but the money arising from the debts so contracted shall be applied to the purpose for which it was raised, or to repay such debts, and to no other purpose whatever." (Article VII, Section 4.)

"Except the debts hereinbefore specified in this article, no debt shall be hereafter contracted by, or on behalf of this State, unless such debt shall be authorized by some law for some single work or object, to be distinctly specified therein; and such law shall impose and provide for the collection of a direct annual tax sufficient to pay the interest on such debt, as it falls due, and also to pay and discharge the principal of such debt, within twenty years from the time of the contracting thereof; but no such law shall take effect until at a general election it shall have been submitted to the people, and have received a majority of all votes cast for and against it at such election; and all money raised by authority of such law, shall be applied only to the specific object therein stated, or to the payment of the debt created thereby; and such law shall be published in at least one newspaper in each County, if one is published therein, throughout the State, for three months preceding the election at which it is submitted to the people." (Article VII, Section 5.)

"The Legislature may, at any time, after the approval of such law by the people, if no debt shall have been contracted in pursuance thereof, repeal the same; and may, at any time, forbid the contracting of any further debt, or liability, under such law; but the tax imposed by such law, in proportion to the debt or liability, which may have been contracted in pursuance thereof, shall remain in force and be irrepealable, and be annually collected, until the principal and interest are fully paid." (Article VII, Section 6.)

KANSAS (1861)

"For the purpose of defraying extraordinary expenses and making public improvements, the state may contract public debts; but such debts shall never, in the aggregate, exceed one million dollars, except as hereinafter provided. Every such debt shall be authorized by law for some purpose specified therein, and the vote of a majority of all the members elected to each house, to be taken by the yeas and nays, shall be necessary to the passage of such law; and every such law shall provide for levying an annual tax sufficient to pay the annual interest of such debt, and the principal thereof, when it shall become due; and shall specifically appropriate the proceeds of such taxes to the payment of such principal and interest; and such appropriation shall not be repealed nor the taxes postponed or diminished, until the interest and principal of such debt shall have been wholly paid." (Article 11, Section 6.)

"No debt shall be contracted by the state except as herein provided, unless the proposed law for creating such debt shall first be submitted to a direct vote of the electors of the state at some general election; and if such proposed law shall be ratified by a majority of all the votes cast at such general election, then it shall be the duty of the legislature next after such election to enact such law and create such debt, subject to all the provisions and restrictions provided in the preceding section of this article." (Article 11, Section 7.)

"The state may borrow money to repel invasion, suppress insurrection, or defend the state in time of war; but the money thus raised, shall be applied exclusively to the object for which the loan was authorized, or to the repayment of the debt thereby created." (Article 11, Section 8.)

"The state shall never be a party in carrying on any work of internal improvement except that it may adopt, construct, reconstruct and maintain a state system of highways, but no general property tax shall ever be laid nor bonds issued by the state for such highways." (Article 11, Section 9, Amended 1920 and 1928.)

KENTUCKY (1891)

"The General Assembly may contract debts to meet casual deficits or failures in the revenue; but such debts, direct or contingent, singly or in the aggregate, shall not at any time exceed five hundred thousand dollars, and the moneys arising from loans creating such debts shall be applied only to the purpose or purposes for which they were obtained, or to repay such debts: Provided, The General Assembly may contract debts to repel invasion, suppress insurrection, or, if hostilities are threatened, provide for the public defense." (Section 49.)

"No act of the General Assembly shall authorize any debt to be contracted on behalf of the Commonwealth except for the purposes mentioned [above] . . . , unless provision be made therein to levy and collect an annual tax sufficient to pay the interest stipulated, and to discharge the debt within thirty years; nor shall such act take effect until it shall have been submitted to the people at a general election, and shall have received a majority of all the votes cast for and against it: Provided, The General Assembly may contract debts by borrowing money to pay any part of the debt of the State, without submission to the people and without making provision in the act authorizing the same for a tax to discharge the debt so contracted, or the interest thereon." (Section 50.)

"All laws authorizing the borrowing of money by and on behalf of the Commonwealth, . . . shall specify the purpose for which the money is to be used, and the money so borrowed shall be used for no other purpose." (Section 178.)

LOUISIANA (1921)

"Whenever, during the interim between sessions of the Legislature, the Board of Liquidation of the State Debt should find and determine that the appropriations for, or revenues of any budget unit of the State are insufficient to care for same adequately, or that an emergency exists, it is hereby authorized and empowered to appropriate from any surplus in the General Fund of the State, as certified by the Treasurer, or to borrow upon the credit of the State, any amount that it may find necessary to care for said budget unit of the State, after having obtained the written consent of a majority of the members elected to each House of the Legislature . . . .

"The maximum amount which may be borrowed and/or appropriated for any budget unit under this authority shall in no event exceed, during any fiscal year, One Hundred Thousand Dollars ($100,000.00); provided, that the total amount which may be borrowed and/or appropriated by the Board of Liquidation of the State Debt under this authority, during any fiscal year, for all budget units shall in no event exceed One Million Dollars ($1,000,000.00); and provided, further, that the total amount of loans under this authority outstanding at any one time shall in no event exceed Two Million Dollars ($2,000,000.00)" (Article IV, Section 1-a, Amendment proclaimed 1944.)

"The Legislature shall have no power to contract or to authorize the contracting of any debt or liability on behalf of the State; or to issue bonds or other evidence of indebtedness thereof, except for the purpose of repelling invasion, or for the suppression of insurrection . . . . " (Article IV, Section 2.)

[Numerous provisions permit the Board of Liquidation of the State Debt to fund into bonds constituting general obligations of the State various monies for different specified purposes. Other provisions provide borrowing authority for the ports of New Orleans and Baton Rouge highway purposes, Orleans Parish schools, penitentiary.]

MAINE (1820)

"The credit of the state shall not be directly or indirectly loaned in any case. The legislature shall not create any debt or debts, liability or liabilities, on behalf of the state, which shall singly, or in the aggregate, with previous debts and liabilities hereafter incurred at any one time, exceed two million dollars, except to suppress insurrection, to repel invasion, or for purposes of war; and excepting also that whenever two-thirds of both houses shall deem it necessary, by proper enactment ratified by a majority of the electors voting thereon at a general or special election, the legislature may authorize the issuance of bonds on behalf of the state at such times and in such amounts and for such purposes as approved by such action; but this shall not be construed to refer to any money that has been, or may be deposited with this state by the government of the United States, or to any fund which the state shall hold in trust for any Indian tribe. Whenever ratification by the electors is essential to the validity of bonds to be issued on behalf of the state, the question submitted to the electors shall be accompanied by a statement setting forth the total amount of bonds of the state outstanding and unpaid, the total amount of bonds of the state authorized and unissued, and the total amount of bonds of the state contemplated to be issued if the enactment submitted to the electors be ratified." (Article LXXV, Section 14, Amendment adopted 1951.)

MARYLAND (1867)

"No debt shall be hereafter contracted by the General Assembly unless such debt shall be authorized by a law providing for the collection of an annual tax or taxes sufficient to pay the interest on such debt as it falls due, and also to discharge the principal thereof within fifteen years from the time of contracting the same; and the taxes laid for this purpose shall not be repealed or applied to any other object until the said debt and interest thereon shall be fully discharged. The credit of the State shall not in any manner be given, or loaned to, or in aid of any individual association or corporation; nor shall the General Assembly have the power in any mode to involve the State in the construction of works of internal improvement, nor in granting any aid thereto which shall involve the faith or credit of the State; nor make any appropriation therefor, except in aid of the Construction of works of internal improvements in the counties of St. Mary's, Charles and Calvert, which have no direct advantage from such works as have been heretofore aided by the State; and provided that such aid, advances or appropriations shall not exceed in the aggregate the sum of five hundred thousand dollars. And they shall not use or appropriate the proceeds of the internal improvement companies, or of the State tax, now levied, or which may hereafter be levied, to pay off the public debt [or] to any other purpose until the interest and debt are fully paid or the sinking fund shall be equal to the amount of the outstanding debt; but the General Assembly may, without laying a tax, borrow an amount never to exceed fifty thousand dollars to meet temporary deficiencies in the Treasury, and may contract debts to any amount that may be necessary for the defense of the State. And provided further that nothing in this section shall be construed to prohibit the raising of funds for the purpose of aiding or compensating in such manner or way as the General Assembly of the State shall deem proper, those citizens of the State who have served, with honor, their Country and State in time of War; provided, however, that such action of the General Assembly shall be effective only when submitted to and approved by a vote of the people of the State at the General Election next following the enactment of such legislation." (Article III, Section 34, Amendment ratified 1924.)

MASSACHUSETTS (1780)

"The commonwealth may borrow money to repel invasion, suppress insurrection, defend the commonwealth, or to assist the United States in case of war, and may also borrow money in anticipation of receipts from taxes or other sources, such loan to be paid out of the revenue of the year in which it is created." (Article LXII, Section 2.)

"In addition to the loans which may be contracted as before provided, the commonwealth may borrow money only by a vote, taken by the yeas and nays, of two-thirds of each house of the general court present and voting thereon. The governor shall recommend to the general court the term for which any loan shall be contracted." (Article LXII, Section 3.)

"Borrowed money shall not be expended for any other purpose than that for which it was borrowed or for the reduction or discharge of the principal of the loan." (Article LXII, Section 4, Amendment adopted 1918.)

MICHIGAN (1909)

"Whenever any question is submitted to a vote of the electors which involves the direct expenditure of public money or the issue of bonds, only such persons having the qualifications of electors who have property assessed for taxes in any part of the district or territory to be affected by the result of such election or the lawful husbands or wives of such persons shall be entitled to vote thereon." (Article III, Section 4.)

"The State may contract debts to meet deficits in revenue, but such debts shall not in the aggregate at any time exceed two hundred fifty thousand dollars. The State may also contract debts to repel invasion, suppress insurrection, defend the State or aid the United States in time of war. The money so raised shall be applied to the purposes for which it is raised or to the payment of the debts contracted . . . . " (Article X, Section 10.)

"No script, certificate or other evidence of state indebtedness shall be issued, except for such debts as are expressly authorized in this constitution." (Article X, Section 11.)

MINNESOTA (1858)

"For the purpose of defraying extraordinary expenditures, the state may contract public debts, but such debts shall never, in the aggregate, exceed two hundred and fifty thousand dollars; every such debt shall be authorized by law, for some single object, to be distinctly specified therein; and no such law shall take effect until it shall have been passed by the vote of two-thirds of the members of each branch of the legislature, to be recorded by yeas and nays on the journals of each house respectively; and every such law shall levy a tax annually sufficient to pay the annual interest of such debt, and also a tax sufficient to pay the principal of such debt within ten years from the final passage of such law, and shall specially appropriate the proceeds of such taxes to the payment of such principal and interest; and such appropriation and taxes shall not be repealed, postponed, or diminished, until the principal and interest of such debt shall have been wholly paid. The state shall never contract any debts for works of internal improvements, or be a party in carrying on such works, except as authorized by . . . this Constitution . . . . " (Article IX, Section 5.)

"All debts authorized by the preceding section shall be contracted by loan on State bonds of amounts not less than five hundred dollars each on interest, payable within ten years after the final passage of the law authorizing such debt; and such bonds shall not be sold by the State under par. A correct registry of all such bonds shall be kept by the treasurer, in numerical order, so as always to exhibit the number and amount unpaid and to whom severally made payable." (Article IX, Section 6.)

"The State shall never contract any public debt, unless in time of war, to repel invasion or suppress insurrection, except in the cases and in the manner provided [above]." (Article IX, Section 7.)

"The money arising from any loan made, or debt or liability contracted, shall be applied to the object specified in the act authorizing such debt or liability, or to the repayment of such debt or liability, and to no other purpose whatever." (Article IX, Section 8.)

Missouri (1945)

"The general assembly shall have no power to contract or authorize the contracting of any liability of the state, or to issue bonds therefor, except (1) to refund outstanding bonds, the refunding bonds to mature not more than twenty-five years from date, (2) on the recommendation of the governor, for a temporary liability to be incurred by reason of unforeseen emergency or casual deficiency in revenue, in a sum not to exceed one million dollars for any one year and to be paid in not more than five years from its creation, and (3) when the liability exceeds one million dollars, the general assembly as on constitutional amendments, or the people by the initiative, may also submit a measure containing the amount, purpose and terms of the liability, and if the measure is approved by a majority of the qualified electors of the state voting thereon at the election, the liability may be incurred, and the bonds issued therefor must be retired serially and by installments within a period not exceeding twenty-five years from their date. Before any bonds are issued under this section the general assembly shall make adequate provision for the payment of the principal and interest, and may provide an annual tax on all taxable property in an amount sufficient for the purpose." (Article III, Section 37.)

Montana (1889)

"The legislative assembly shall not in any manner create any debt except by law which shall be irrepealable until the indebtedness therein provided for shall have been fully paid or discharged; such law shall specify the purpose to which the funds so raised shall be applied and provide for the levy of a tax sufficient to pay the interest on, and extinguish the principal of such debt within the time limited by such law for the payment thereof; but no debt or liability shall be created which shall singly, or in the aggregate with any existing debt or liability, exceed the sum of one hundred thousand dollars ($100,000) except in the case of war, to repel invasion or suppress insurrection, unless the law authorizing the same shall have been submitted to the people at a general election and shall have received a majority of the votes cast for and against it at such election." (Article XIII, Section 2.)

Nebraska (1875)

"The state may, to meet casual deficits, or failures in the revenues, contract debts never to exceed in the aggregate one hundred thousand dollars, and no greater indebtedness shall be incurred except for the purpose of repelling invasion, suppressing insurrection, or defending the state in war, and provision shall be made for the payment of the interest annually, as it shall accrue, by a tax levied for the purpose, or from other sources of revenue, which law providing for the payment of such interest by such tax shall be irrepealable until such debt be paid." (Article VIII, Section 1.)

NEVADA (1864)

"The state may contract public debts; but such debts shall never, in the aggregate, exclusive of interest, exceed the sum of one per cent of the assessed valuation of the state, as shown by the reports of the county assessors to the state controller, except for the purpose of defraying extraordinary expenses, as hereinafter mentioned. Every such debt shall be authorized by law for some purpose or purposes, to be distinctly specified therein; and every such law shall provide for levying an annual tax sufficient to pay the interest semiannually, and the principal within twenty years from the passage of such law, and shall specially appropriate the proceeds of said taxes to the payment of said principal and interest; and such appropriation shall not be repealed nor the taxes postponed or diminished until the principal and interest of said debts shall have been wholly paid. Every contract of indebtedness entered into or assumed by or on behalf of the state, when all its debts and liabilities amount to said sum before mentioned, shall be void and of no effect, except in cases of money borrowed to repel invasion, suppress insurrection, defend the state in time of war, or, if hostilities be threatened, provide for the public defense.

"The state, notwithstanding the foregoing limitations, may, pursuant to authority of the legislature, make and enter into any and all contracts necessary, expedient or advisable for the protection and preservation of any of its property or natural resources, or for the purposes of obtaining the benefits thereof, however arising and whether arising by or through any undertaking or project of the United States or by or through any treaty or compact between the states, or otherwise. The legislature may from time to time make such appropriations as may be necessary to carry out the obligations of the state under such contracts, and shall levy such tax as may be necessary to pay the same or carry them into eflect." (Article IX, Section 3, Amendment ratified 1916 and 1934.)

NEW JERSEY (1948)

"The Legislature shall not, in any manner create in any fiscal year a debt or debts, liability or liabilities of the State, which together with any previous debts or liabilities shall exceed at any time one per centum of the total amount appropriated by the general appropriation law for that fiscal year, unless the same shall be authorized by a law for some single object or work distinctly specified therein. Regardless of any limitation relating to taxation in this Constitution, such law shall provide the ways and means, exclusive of loans, to pay the interest of such debt or liability as it falls due, and also to pay and discharge the principal thereof within thirty-five years from the time it is contracted; and the law shall not be repealed until such debt or liability and the interest thereon are fully paid and discharged. No such law shall take effect until it shall have been submitted to the people at a general election and approved by a majority of the legally qualified voters of the State voting thereon. All money to be raised by the authority of such law shall be applied only to the specific object stated therein, and to the payment of the debt thereby created. This paragraph shall not be construed to refer to any money that has been or may be deposited with this State by the government of the United States. Nor shall anything in this paragraph contained apply to the creation of any debts or liabilities for purposes of war, or to repel invasion, or to suppress insurrection or to meet an emergency caused by disaster or act of God." (Article VIII, Section II, Paragraph 3.)

NEW MEXICO (1911)

"The State may borrow money not exceeding the sum of two hundred thousand dollars in the aggregate to meet casual deficits or failure in revenue, or for necessary expenses. The state may also contract debts to suppress insurrection and to provide for the public defense." (Article IX, Section 7.)

"No debt other than those specified in the preceding section shall be contracted by or on behalf of this State, unless authorized by law for some specified work or object; which law shall provide for an annual tax levy sufficient to pay the interest and to provide a sinking fund to pay the principal of such debt within fifty years from the time of the contracting thereof. No such law shall take effect until it shall have been submitted to the qualified electors of the State and have received a majority of all the votes cast thereon at a general election; such law shall be published in full in at least one newspaper in each county of the State, if one be published therein, once each week, for four successive weeks next preceding such election. No debt shall be so created if the total indebtedness of the State, exclusive of the debts of the Territory, and the several counties thereof, assumed by the State, would thereby be made to exceed one per centum of the assessed valuation of all the property subject to taxation in the State as shown by the preceding general assessment." (Article IX, Section 8.)

"Any money borrowed by the state, . . . shall be applied to the purpose for which it was obtained, or to repay such loan, and to no other purpose whatever." (Article IX, Section 9.)

NEW YORK (1938)

"The state may contract debts in anticipation of the receipt of taxes and revenues, direct or indirect, for the purposes and within the amounts of appropriations theretofore made. Notes or other obligations for the moneys so borrowed shall be issued as may be provided by law, and shall with the interest thereon be paid from such taxes and revenues within one year from the date of issue.

"The state may also contract debts in anticipation of the receipt of the proceeds of the sale of bonds theretofore authorized, for the purpose and within the amounts of the bonds so authorized. Notes or obligations for the money so borrowed shall be issued as may be provided by law, and shall with the interest thereon be paid from the proceeds of the sale of such bonds within two years from the date of issue." (Article VII, Section 9.)

"In addition to the above limited power to contract debts, the state may contract debts to repel invasion, suppress insurrection, or defend the state in war, or to suppress forest fires; but the money arising from the contracting of such debts shall be applied for the purpose for which it was raised, or to repay such debts, and to no other purpose whatever." (Article VII, Section 10.)

"Except the debts specified [above] . . . , no debt shall be hereafter contracted by or in behalf of the state, unless such debt shall be authorized by law, for some single work or purpose, to be distinctly specified therein. No such law shall take effect until it shall, at a general election, have been submitted to the people, and have received a majority of all the votes cast for and against it at such election nor shall it be submitted to be voted on within three months after its passage nor at any general election when any other law or any bill shall be submitted to be voted for or against.

"The legislature may, at any time after the approval of such law by the people, if no debt shall have been contracted in pursuance thereof, repeal the same; and may at any time, by law, forbid the contracting of any further debt or liability under such law." (Article VII, Section 11.)

"Except the debts specified [above] . . . , all debts contracted by the state and each portion of any such debt from time to time so contracted shall be paid in equal annual installments, the first of which shall be payable not more than one year, and the last of which shall be payable not more than forty years, after such debt or portion thereof shall have been contracted, provided, however, that in contracting any such debt the privilege of paying all or any part of such debt prior to the date on which the same shall be due may be reserved to the state in such manner as may be provided by law. No such debt shall be contracted for a period longer than that of the probable life of the work or purpose for which the debt is to be contracted, to be determined by general laws, which determination shall be conclusive.

"The money arising from any loan creating such debt or liability shall be applied only to the work or purpose specified in the act authorizing such debt or liability, or for the payment of such debt or liability, including any notes or obligations issued in anticipation of the sale of bonds evidencing such debt or liability." (Article VII, Section 12.)

"The legislature may provide means and authority whereby any state debt may be refunded if, when it was contracted, the privilege to pay prior to the date payable was reserved to the state and provided that the debt as thus refunded shall be paid in equal annual installments which shall be not less in amount than the required annual installments of the debt so refunded." (Article VII, Section 13.)

"The legislature shall annually provide by appropriation for the payment of the interest upon and installments of principal of all debts created on behalf of the state except those contracted under section 9 of this article, as the same shall fall due, and for the contribution to all of the sinking funds heretofore created by law, of the amounts annually to be contributed under the provisions . . . of this article. If at any time the legislature shall fail to make any such appropriation, the comptroller shall set apart from the first revenues thereafter received, applicable to the general fund of the state, a sum sufficient to pay such interest, installments of principal, or contributions to such sinking fund, as the case may be, and shall so apply the moneys thus set apart. The comptroller may be required to set aside and apply such revenues as aforesaid, at the suit of any holder of such bonds." (Article VII, Section 16.)

NORTH CAROLINA (1876)

"The General Assembly shall have the power to contract debts and to pledge the faith and credit of the State . . . for the following purposes: To fund or refund a valid existing debt; to borrow in anticipation of the collection of taxes due and payable within the fiscal year to an amount not exceeding fifty per centum of such taxes; to supply a casual deficit; to suppress riots or insurrections, or to repel invasions. For any purpose other than these enumerated, the General Assembly shall have no power, during any biennium, to contract new debts on behalf of the State to an amount in excess of two-thirds of the amount by which the State's outstanding indebtedness shall have been reduced during the next preceding biennium, unless the subject be submitted to a vote of the people of the State; . . . and for any purpose other than these enumerated the General Assembly shall have no power to authorize counties or municipalities to contract debts. . . . In any election held in the State . . . under the provisions of this section, the proposed indebtedness must be approved by a majority of those who shall vote thereon . . . " (Article V, Section 4.)

NORTH DAKOTA (1889)

"The state may issue or guarantee the payment of bonds, provided that all bonds in excess of two million dollars shall be secured by first mortgage upon real estate in amounts not to exceed one-half of its value; or upon real and personal property of state owned utilities, enterprises or industries, in amounts not exceeding its value, and provided further, that the state shall not issue or guarantee bonds upon property of state owned utilities, enterprises or industries in excess of ten million dollars.

"No further indebtedness shall be incurred by the state unless evidenced by a bond issue, which shall be authorized by law for certain purposes to be clearly defined. Every law authorizing a bond issue shall provide for levying an annual tax, or make other provision, sufficient to pay the interest semi-annually, and the principal within thirty years from the date of the issue of such bonds and shall specially appropriate the proceeds of such tax, or of such other provisions to the payment of said principal and interest, and such appropriation shall not be repealed nor the tax or other provisions discontinued until such debt, both principal and interest, shall have been paid. No debt in excess of the limit named herein shall be incurred except for the purpose of repelling invasion, suppressing insurrection, defending the state in time of war or to provide for the public defense in case of threatened hostilities." (Article 42, Section 182, Amendment adopted 1924.)

OHIO (1851)

The State may contract debts, to supply casual deficits or failures in revenues, or to meet expenses not otherwise provided for; but the aggregate amount of such debts, direct and contingent, whether contracted by virtue of one or more acts of the General Assembly, or at different periods of time, shall never exceed seven hundred and fifty thousand dollars; and the money, arising from the creation of such debts, shall be applied to the purpose for which it was obtained, or to repay the debts so contracted, and to no other purpose whatever." (Article VIII, Section 1.)

"In addition to the above limited power, the State may contract debts to repel invasion, suppress insurrection, defend the State in war, or to redeem the present outstanding indebtedness of the State; but the money, arising from the contracting of such debts, shall be applied to the purpose for which it was raised, or to repay such debts, and to no other purpose whatever; and all debts, incurred to redeem the present outstanding indebtedness of the State, shall be so contracted as to be payable by the sinking fund, hereinafter provided for, as the same shall accumulate." (Article VIII, Section 2.)

"Except the debts above specified in sections one and two of this article, no debt whatever shall hereafter be created by or on behalf of the State." (Article VIII, Section 3.)

"The credit of the State shall not, in any manner, be given or loaned to, or in aid of, any individual association or corporation whatever . . . . " (Article VIII, Section 4.)

"The faith of the State being pledged for the payment of its public debt, in order to provide therefor, there shall be created a sinking fund, which shall be sufficient to pay the accruing interest on such debt, and, annually, to reduce the principal thereof, by a sum not less than one hundred thousand dollars, increased yearly, and each and every year, by compounding, at the rate of six per cent per annum. The said sinking fund shall consist, of the net annual income of the public works and stocks owned by the State, of any other further funds or resources that are, or may be, provided by law, and of such further sum, to be raised by taxation, as may be required for the purposes aforesaid." (Article VIII, Section 7.)

"Except as otherwise provided in this constitution the state shall never contract any debt for purposes of internal improvement." (Article XII, Section 6, Amendment adopted 1912.)

"No bonded indebtedness of the state, or any political sub-divisions thereof, shall be incurred or renewed, unless, in the legislation under which such indebtedness is incurred or renewed, provision is made for levying and collecting annually by taxation an amount sufficient to pay the interest on said bonds, and to provide a sinking fund for their final redemption at maturity." (Article XII, Section 11, Amendment adopted 1912.)

OKLAHOMA (1907)

"For the purpose of paying the State debt, if any, the Legislature shall provide for levying a tax, annually, sufficient to pay the annual interest and principal of such debt within twenty-five years from the final passage of the law creating the debt." (Article X, Section 4.)

" . . . the Governor may in his discretion issue a deficiency certificate or certificates to the State Auditor for the benefit of any department, institution, or agency of the State, if the amount of such deficiency certificate or certificates be within the limit of the current appropriation for that department, institution, or agency, whereupon the State Auditor shall issue warrants to the extent of such certificate or certificates for the payment of such claims as may be authorized by the Governor, and such warrants shall become a part of the public debt and shall be paid out of any money appropriated by the Legislature and made lawfully available therefor; Provided, Further, that in no event shall said deficiency certificate or certificates exceed in the aggregate the sum of Five Hundred Thousand ($500,000.00) Dollars in any fiscal year.

"The State shall never create or authorize the creation of any debt or obligation, or fund or pay any deficit, against the State, or any department, institution or agency thereof, regardless of its form or source of money from which it is to be paid, except as provided [elsewhere] . . . Provided, that the Legislature may fund or refund the State debt arising prior to July 1, 1941." (Article X, Section 23, Amendment adopted 1941.)

"Any surplus which has accrued or may hereafter accrue to the General Revenue Fund of the State of Oklahoma during any fiscal year shall be placed monthly in a sinking fund in the State Treasury to be used solely for the purpose of paying the principal and interest of the outstanding and unpaid bonded indebtedness of the State of Oklahoma . . . . " (Article X, Section 23a, Amendment adopted 1944.)

"In addition to the above limited power to contract debts, the State may contract debts to repel invasion, suppress insurrection or to defend the State in war; but the money arising from the contracting of such debts shall be applied to the purpose for which it was raised, or to repay such debts, and to no other purpose whatever." (Article X, Section 24.)

"Except the debts specified [above] . . . no debts shall hereafter be contracted by or on behalf of this State unless such debts shall be authorized by law for some work or object, to be distinctly specified therein; and such law shall impose and provide for the collection of a direct annual tax to pay, and sufficient to pay, the interest on such debt as it falls due, and also to pay and discharge the principal of such

debt within twenty-five years from the time of the contracting thereof.
No such law shall take effect until it shall, at a general election, have
been submitted to the people and have received a majority of all the
votes cast for and against it at such election. On the final passage of
such bill in either House of the Legislature, the question shall be by
yeas and nays, to be duly entered on the journals thereof, and shall be:
'Shall this bill pass, and ought the same to receive the sanction of the
people?' " (Article X, Section 25.)

"No bond or evidence of indebtedness of this State shall be valid
unless the same shall have endorsed thereon a certificate, signed by the
Auditor and Attorney General of the State, showing that the bond or
evidence of debt is issued pursuant to law and is within the debt
limit . . . . " (Article X, Section 29.)

OREGON (1859)

"The legislative assembly shall not lend the credit of the state nor
in any manner create any debt or liabilities which shall singly or in
the aggregate with previous debts or liabilities exceed the sum of fifty
thousand dollars, except in case of war or to repel invasion or to suppress insurrection . . . , every contract of indebtedness entered into or
assumed by or on behalf of the state in violation of the provisions of
this section shall be void and of no effect." (Article XI, Section 7,
Amendment adopted 1920.)

"Refunding bonds may be issued and sold to refund any bonds
issued under authority of sections 1 and 2 of this article. There may
be issued and outstanding at any one time bonds aggregating the
amount authorized by section 1 hereof, but at no time shall the total
of all bonds outstanding, including refunding bonds, exceed the
amount so authorized." (Article XI, A, Section 6, Amendment adopted
1950.)

PENNSYLVANIA (1874)

"No debt shall be created by or on behalf of the State except to
supply casual deficiencies of revenue, repel invasion, suppress insurrection, defend the State in war, or to pay existing debt; and the debt
created to supply deficiencies in revenue shall never exceed in the
aggregate, at any one time, one million dollars . . . . " (Article IX,
Section 4, Amendment adopted 1923.)

"All laws, authorizing the borrowing of money by and on behalf of
the State, shall specify the purpose for which the money is to be used,
and the money so borrowed shall be used for the purpose specified
and no other." (Article IX, Section 5.)

"To provide for the payment of the present State debt, and any additional debt contracted as aforesaid, the General Assembly shall continue and maintain the sinking fund, sufficient to pay the accruing interest on such debt and annually to reduce the principal thereof by a sum not less than two hundred and fifty thousand dollars; the said sinking fund shall consist of the proceeds of the sale of the public works or any part thereof, and of the income or proceeds of the sale of any stocks owned by the Commonwealth, together with other funds and resources that may be designated by law, and shall be increased from time to time by assigning to it any part of the taxes or other revenue of the State not required for the ordinary and current expenses of government; and unless in case of war, invasion or insurrection, no part of the said sinking fund shall be used or applied otherwise than in the extinguishment of the public debt." (Article IX, Section 11.)

"The moneys of the State, over and above the necessary reserve, shall be used in the payment of the debt of the State, either directly or through the sinking fund, and the moneys of the sinking fund shall never be invested in or loaned upon the security of anything, except the bonds of the United States or of this State." (Article IX, Section 12.)

RHODE ISLAND (1843)

"The general assembly shall have no powers, hereafter, without the express consent of the people, to incur state debts to an amount exceeding fifty thousand dollars, except in time of war, or in case of insurrection or invasion; nor shall they in any case, without such consent, pledge the faith of the state for the payment of the obligations of others. This section shall not be construed to refer to any money that may be deposited with this state by the government of the United States." (Article XXXI, Section 1, Amendment adopted 1951.)

"Notwithstanding the provisions of section 1 of this article the general assembly may provide by law for the state to borrow in any fiscal year, in anticipation of receipts from taxes, sums of money not exceeding twenty percent of the receipts from taxes during the next prior fiscal year, and, in anticipation of receipts from other sources, additional sums of money, not exceeding ten percent of the receipts from such other sources during the said next prior fiscal year; provided, that the aggregate of all such borrowings shall not exceed a sum equal to thirty percent of the actual receipts from taxes during the said next prior fiscal year. Any money so borrowed in anticipation of such receipts shall be repaid within the fiscal year of the state in which such borrowings take place. No money shall be so borrowed in anticipation of such receipts in any fiscal year until all money so borrowed in all previous fiscal years shall have been repaid." (Article XXXI, Section 2, Amendment adopted 1951.)

SOUTH CAROLINA (1895)

"To the end that the public debt of South Carolina may not hereafter be increased without the due consideration and free consent of the people of the State, the General Assembly is hereby forbidden to create any further debt or obligation, either by the loan of the credit of the State, by guaranty, endorsement or otherwise, except for the ordinary and current business of the State, without first submitting the question as to the creation of such new debt, guaranty, endorsement or loan of its credit to the qualified electors of this State at a general State election; and unless two-thirds of the qualified electors of this State, voting on the question, shall be in favor of increasing the debt, guaranty, endorsement, or loan of its credit, none shall be created or made. And any debt contracted by the State shall be by loan on State bonds, of amounts not less than fifty dollars each, bearing interest, payable not more than forty years after final passage of the law authorizing such debt. A correct registry of all such bonds shall be kept by the Treasurer in numerical order, so as to always exhibit the number and amount unpaid, and to whom severally made payable. And the General Assembly shall levy an annual tax sufficient to pay the annual interest on said bonds." (Article X, Section 11.)

SOUTH DAKOTA (1889)

"For the purpose of developing the resources and improving the economic facilities of South Dakota, the state may engage in works of internal improvement, may own and conduct proper business enterprises, may loan or give its credit to, or in aid of, any association, or corporation, organized for such purposes. But any such association or corporation shall be subject to regulation and control by the state as may be provided by law. No money of the state shall be appropriated, or indebtedness incurred for any of the purposes of this section, except by the vote of two-thirds of the members of each branch of the legislature. The state may also assume or pay any debt or liability incurred in time of war for the defense of this state. The state may establish and maintain a system of rural credits and thereby loan and extend credit to the people of the state upon real estate security in such manner and upon such terms and conditions as may be prescribed by general law. The limit of indebtedness contained [below] . . . shall not apply to the provisions of this section, but the indebtedness of the state for the purposes contained in this section shall never exceed one-half of one per cent of the assessed valuations of the property of the state, provided, however, that nothing contained in this section shall affect the refinancing or refunding of the present outstanding indebtedness of this state." (Article XIII, Section 1.)

"For the purpose of defraying extraordinary expenses and making public improvements, or to meet casual deficits or failure in revenue, the state may contract debts never to exceed with previous debts in the aggregate one hundred thousand dollars, and no greater indebtedness shall be incurred except for the purpose of repelling invasion, suppressing insurrection, or defending the state or the United States in war and provision shall be made by law for the payment of the interest annually, and the principal when due, by tax levied for the purpose or from other sources of revenue; which law providing for the payment of such interest and principal by such tax or otherwise shall be irrepealable until such debt is paid: Provided, however, the state of South Dakota shall have the power to refund the territorial debt assumed by the state of South Dakota, by bonds of the state of South Dakota." (Article XIII, Section 2.)

TEXAS (1876)

"No debt shall be created by or on behalf of the State, except to supply casual deficiencies of revenue, repel invasion, suppress insurrection, defend the State in war, or pay existing debt; and the debt created to supply deficiencies in the revenue, shall never exceed in the aggregate at any one time two hundred thousand dollars." (Article III, Section 49.)

UTAH (1896)

"To meet casual deficits or failures in revenue, and for necessary expenditures for public purposes, including the erection of public buildings, and for the payment of all Territorial indebtedness assumed by the State, the State may contract debts, not exceeding in the aggregate at any one time, an amount equal to one and one-half per centum of the value of the taxable property of the State, as shown by the last assessment for State purposes, previous to the incurring of such indebtedness. But the state shall never contract any indebtedness, except as in the next Section provided, in excess of such amount, and all monies arising from loans herein authorized, shall be applied solely to the purposes for which they were obtained." (Article XIV, Section 1, Amended 1910.)

"The State may contract debts to repel invasion, suppress insurrection, or to defend the State in war, but the money arising from the contracting of such debts shall be applied solely to the purpose for which it was obtained." (Article XIV, Section 2.)

"All monies borrowed by, or on behalf of the State or any legal subdivision thereof, shall be used solely for the purpose specified in the law authorizing the loan." (Article XIV, Section 5.)

VIRGINIA (1928)

"The General Assembly may contract debts to meet casual deficits in revenue, to redeem a previous liability of the State, to suppress insurrection, repel invasion, or defend the State in time of war." (Article XIII, Section 184.)

"No debt or liability, except the debts specified . . . [above], shall be hereafter contracted by or in behalf of the State, unless such debt shall be authorized by law for some single purpose constituting new capital outlay, to be distinctly specified therein, and a vote of a majority of all the members elected to each house shall be necessary to the passage of such law. On the final passage of such law in either house of the General Assembly, the question shall be taken by ayes and noes, to be duly entered on the journals thereof, and shall be 'Shall this bill pass, and ought the same to receive the sanction of the people?' No such law shall take effect until it shall have been submitted to the people at a general election, and shall have received a majority of all the votes cast for or against it. Such law shall be published, as may be prescribed by law, for at least three months next preceding such election.

"The aggregate amount of the debts authorized by this section shall not at any time exceed one per centum of the assessed value of all the taxable real estate in the State, as shown by the last preceding assessment.

"None of the provisions of this section shall apply to the debts specifically authorized by [the preceding] . . . . " (Article XIII, Section 184-a.)

" . . . Every law hereafter enacted by the General Assembly creating a debt or authorizing a loan, shall provide for the creation and maintenance of a sinking fund for the payment or redemption of the same." (Article XIII, Section 7.)

WASHINGTON (1889)

"The state may to meet casual deficits or failure in revenues, or for expenses not provided for, contract debts, but such debts, direct and contingent, singly or in the aggregate, shall not at any time exceed four hundred thousand dollars ($400,000), and the moneys arising from the loans creating such debts shall be applied to the purpose for which they were obtained or to repay the debts so contracted, and to no other purpose whatever." (Article VIII, Section 1.)

"In addition to the above, limited power to contract debts the state may contract debts to repel invasion, suppress insurrection, or to defend the state in war, but the money arising from the contracting of such debts shall be applied to the purpose for which it was raised and to no other purpose whatever." (Article VIII, Section 2.)

"Except the debt specified . . . [above], no debts shall hereafter be contracted by, or on behalf of this state, unless such debt shall be authorized by law for some single work or object to be distinctly specified therein, which law shall provide ways and means, exclusive of loans, for the payment of the interest on such debt as it falls due, and also to pay and discharge the principal of such debt within twenty years from the time of the contracting thereof. No such law shall take effect until it shall, at a general election, have been submitted to the people and have received a majority of all the votes cast for and against it at such election, and all moneys raised by authority of such law shall be applied only to the specific object therein stated, or to the payment of the debt thereby created, and such law shall be published in at least one newspaper in each county, if one be published therein, throughout the state, for three months next preceding the election at which it is submitted to the people." (Article VIII, Section 3.)

WEST VIRGINIA (1872)

"No debt shall be contracted by this State, except to meet casual deficits in the revenue, to redeem a previous liability of the State, to suppress insurrection, repel invasion or defend the State in time of war; but the payment of any liability other than that for the ordinary expenses of the State, shall be equally distributed over a period of at least twenty years." (Article X, Section 4.)

WISCONSIN (1848)

"For the purpose of defraying extraordinary expenditures the state may contract public debts (but such debts shall never in the aggregate exceed one hundred thousand dollars). Every such debt shall be authorized by law, for some purpose or purposes to be distinctly specified therein; and the vote of a majority of all the members elected to each house, to be taken by yeas and nays, shall be necessary to the passage of such law; and every such law shall provide for levying an annual tax sufficient to pay the annual interest of such debt and the principal within five years from the passage of such law, and shall specially appropriate the proceeds of such taxes to the payment of such principal and interest; and such appropriation shall not be repealed, nor the taxes be postponed or diminished, until the principal and interest of such debt shall have been wholly paid." (Article VIII, Section 6.)

"The legislature may also borrow money to repel invasion, suppress insurrection, or defend the state in time of war; but the money thus raised shall be applied exclusively to the object for which the loan was authorized, or to the repayment of the debt thereby created." (Article VIII, Section 7.)

WYOMING (1890)

"The State of Wyoming shall not, in any manner, create any indebtedness exceeding one per centum on the assessed value of the taxable property in the state, as shown by the last general assessment for taxation, preceding; except to suppress insurrection or to provide for the public defense." (Article XVI, Section 1.)

"No debt in excess of the taxes for the current year, shall in any manner be created in the State of Wyoming, unless the proposition to create such debt shall have been submitted to a vote of the people and by them approved; except to suppress insurrection or to provide for the public defense." (Article XVI, Section 2.)

"No bond or evidence of indebtedness of the state shall be valid unless the same shall have endorsed thereon a certificate signed by the auditor and secretary of state that the bond or evidence of debt is issued pursuant to law and is within the debt limit . . . . " (Article XVI, Section 8.)

Appendix B

COURT DECISIONS ON CIRCUMVENTION OF CONSTITUTIONAL DEBT PROVISIONS*

A. Indirect, Contingent, or Assumed Debts

The constitutional debt provision applies only to the state as a corporation, as a political soverign, represented by lawmaking power. The debt restriction does not prevent the state from authorizing counties or municipal corporations to create debts, when the state debt is up to the constitutional limit (*California*—1).

A statute providing for county and city issuance of bonds for poor relief is not unconstitutional as authorizing the creation of state debt (*Ohio*—2). Improvement of county roads where the state is not a party to the improvement, is valid (*Kansas*—3). But the state cannot directly, or indirectly or contingently, pay, or be obligated to pay, all or part of the principal or interest on bonds issued by a drainage district (*Florida*—4).

Money collected by the state for the public school fund, to be disbursed to counties or county school boards, is not part of the state's floating debt, for the payment of which tax proceeds are held in trust and pledged to create a sinking fund (*Alabama*—5). A law which levies a special gas tax and appropriates the proceeds to reimburse counties and special road districts for state road construction does not violate the constitution (*Florida*—6). A statute apportioning the motor fuel tax fund among counties creates no debt against the state but merely appropriates and directs the expenditure of funds collected (*Idaho*—7). A statute authorizing reimbursement to counties for moneys advanced for road construction, from a special fund consisting of the gasoline tax, automobile license tax, and federal aid, does not violate the constitution (*South Carolina*—8).

A statute donating to a flood control district half the state's ad valorem taxes collected in the county, and providing for the taxes to be used in the district to prevent floods and construct improvements

* Taken from The Tax Foundation, *Constitutional Debt Control in the States*, Appendix III-C. States adopting the various rules are shown in parentheses for easy reference; numerals refer to endnotes to Appendix B which cite the specific court decisions.

121

to control flood waters in the county, does not violate the constitutional prohibition against creation of state debt (*Texas*—9). A statute appropriating state taxes to a city where much of the private and public property was destroyed by fire, to be used by the city in payment of interest on bonds to be issued for the reconstruction of public property, and providing a sinking fund for the retirement of the bonds, is not a violation (*Oregon*—10). But a state cannot issue bonds for the acquisition, maintenance, improvement, or extension of a municipal utility or facility (*Florida*—11).

A statute proposing state assumption of indebtedness due the counties for highway construction does not violate the constitutional limit on the power to increase the state's bonded debt (*Georgia*—12). Proposed bonds to be issued by a State Improvement Commission under an arrangement with the state road department, whereby a road is leased to the road department, are not invalid as "state bonds," where the proceeds of a gasoline tax accruing to the county in which the road is located will be used to pay the bonds (*Florida*—13). Obligations incurred by the state, through its highway commission, to a county which advances money or funds for highway construction are debts to which the constitutional provision applies to the extent of the sums advanced (*Kentucky*—14).

A statute providing for the issuance of state general obligation bonds to finance a program of school building construction and other school facilities, enacting a retail sales and use tax, and pledging the resulting revenue to retire the bonds, does not lend or pledge the credit of the state for the benefit of any individual, company, association, or corporation in violation of the constitution (*South Carolina*—15).

A statute authorizing the state board of education to make loans from the permanent fund to the state school equalizing fund and issue certificates of indebtedness does not violate the constitution; there is no pledge of the state's full faith or credit, nor any of its revenues (*Arkansas*—16). While the permanent school fund may be loaned so that interest will accrue, it may not be borrowed upon the state's credit so that the resources or revenues of the state are pledged, directly or indirectly, for repayment (*Arkansas*—17).

Provisions of university student dormitory revenue certificates and a resolution of the board of education authorizing their issuance do not constitute a pledge or loan of the state's credit to an individual, company, corporation, or association. It is not material that individual university students may receive private benefits from construction of the dormitories, and the lessees of the dormitories may obtain legal title thereto under restrictions placing control of the property in the university (*Florida*—18).

A constitutional provision that prohibits giving or lending the state's credit to third persons, individual or corporate, does not affect the mandatory provisions of the constitution as to maintenance of a state-wide school system by legislative enactment (*North Carolina*—19).

A statute approved by vote of the people, providing for the issuance and sale of state bonds for the purpose of lending the proceeds on a mortgage to help war veterans provide homes for themselves, pledges the state's credit for a public purpose and is valid exercise of statutory authority (*North Carolina*—20).

A statute relating to the irrigation and reclamation of certain lands, under which the state is to be paid for the water rights, provides for a state project for a public purpose. It does not contravene the constitutional prohibition against lending the state's credit (*Oregon* —21).

Laws authorizing bonds to aid railroads were not repugnant to early constitutions (*Kansas*—22). Nowadays, legislatures have no power to contract debt, without a vote of the people, to aid in the construction of a railroad or to build a new railroad (*North Carolina*—23). Indorsement of railroad bonds makes the bonds part of the public debt (*Georgia*—24).

B. AUTHORITIES, BOARDS AND COMMISSIONS

The debts of a public corporation or quasi-corporation are not debts against the state. When a state corporation is set up to perform an important public purpose, it can be given power to create a debt on its own account without any liability or debt being imposed on the state. But a fictitious corporation cannot be given power by the legislature to create debt or evade the requirements of the constitution (*Alabama*—25).

Ordinarily, the creation of a state board or commission which requires the appropriation of public funds to carry out its purposes is not treated as the creation of debt, although future appropriations are necessarily contemplated from year to year for an indefinite period (*West Virginia*—26).

On the other hand, the managing officers of the benevolent and penal institutions of a state have no power to contract debts in excess of the appropriations made for the support and operation of the institutions under their charge. A debt against one of these institutions is a debt against the state (*Wisconsin*—27).

1. *Highways*

A statute creating a state highway corporation and authorizing it to issue bonds for public road purposes, which will not constitute a debt of the state, or involve or pledge the faith and credit of the state, to obtain funds to match federal funds for like purposes, does not violate the constitution (*Alabama*—28). Similarly, obligations incurred by the state highway department in the construction, reconstruction, repair, and maintenance of public highways are not subject to the constitutional debt limitation (*North Dakota*—29).

2. *Bridges*

A statute creating a state bridge commission and defining its powers and duties in the purchase, construction, and improvement of public bridges over navigable streams, in and bordering the state, does not violate the constitution (*West Virginia*—30). A law creating a bridge authority to free highways of toll bridges, providing for the issuance of bonds by the authority, pledging surplus funds appropriated to the highways for the purposes of the law, and stating that the state would not be liable for any authority indebtedness, does not violate the constitution (*Alabama*—31).

The creation of an overseas road and toll bridge district with a provision donating to it the right of way over state-owned lands does not impose liability on the state for bonds issued by the district under the statute (*Florida*—32). But a state highway commission in bonding toll bridges on the public highways cannot pledge the commission's credit as security for the bonds (*Kentucky*—33).

3. *Education*

Bonds issued by a state university are not obligations of the state and are not subject to the constitutional debt provision (*Georgia*—34, *New Mexico*—35). Consequently, debt for the following purposes, incurred by state colleges, has been held constitutional: laundry and dry-cleaning service at reduced prices for student benefit (*Georgia*—36), safeguarding military equipment (*Washington*—37), agricultural experiment stations (*Kentucky*—38).

To the contrary, it has been held that a state university is not an independent legal entity but an administrative agency vested by the legislature with certain corporate powers. Any indebtedness authorized by statute is "indebtedness of the state" within the meaning of the constitution (*Oregon*—39). Furthermore, although appropriations for buildings and current expenses of a state educational institution are not indebtedness, appropriations cannot be made that would create a deficit over the constitutional limit (*Kentucky*—40).

4. *Public Buildings*

A proposed bill to create a public corporation with power to erect an office building to be leased to state departments on annual agreements, which does not contemplate appropriations for future years, does not violate the constitution (*Alabama*—41). A statute directing the issuance and sale of bonds by the state board of examiners for the erection of necessary buildings at a state hospital for the insane is not contrary to the constitution (*Montana*—42). Bonds authorized to be issued by a housing authority are not considered indebtedness within the constitutional limitation (*Montana*—43).

However, other cases hold differently. A law providing for a political and corporate body with corporate succession, to acquire, construct, furnish and operate building facilities for the use of the state, and whose only income is to be rentals to be paid by the state for the purpose of paying the body's expenses, violates the constitution (*New Jersey*—44). The state board of control is not authorized to issue certificates of indebtedness covering the cost of acquiring or constructing transmission lines for electrical energy for state buildings (*Oregon*—45).

Under one contemplated transaction the board of commissioners of state institutions was to obtain a loan or advance from the federal government for the erection of buildings at the state insane hospital and state prison. The board would either lease or deed outright to the federal government the land upon which the proposed project would be erected. The board would enter a lease agreement under which the state would pay monthly or annual installments to the federal government for not more than 30 years, until up to 70 percent of the loan or advance was repaid. This created an interest-bearing contract obligation to pay state funds in the future in violation of the constitution (*Florida*—46).

5. *Water-Resource Development*

The full faith, credit, and taxing powers of the state or any of its political subdivisions cannot be pledged, either directly or contingently, for the payment of obligations issued by a public authority in the construction of a hydroelectric and navigation project. The authority's obligation to complete and operate the project does not create a state debt where the law creating the authority and the bonds that are issued provide that no debt of the state is to be created nor is the full faith, credit and taxing power of the state pledged to payment of the authority's obligations. This is true irrespective of whether the amount available is sufficient to construct the project or whether the revenues to be derived therefrom are sufficient to retire the obligations (*South Carolina*—47).

A statutory conservation district set up as an authority in one state was at first held not a "political subdivision of the state" within the constitutional provision, but a governmental agency of the state governed in its debt features by the constitution (*Oklahoma*—48). Later, however, the authority, created without appropriation of state revenues and operating on revenues not wholly or partly derived through the state's taxing power, by reasons of its adjudicated status as a self-liquidating governmental agency, was held not within the class of "agencies of the state" whose power to incur indebtedness of its own will or under state authority is restricted by the constitution. The authority has power to issue and sell bonds (*Oklahoma*—49). A constitutional amendment prohibiting the incurring of indebtedness by state agencies does not nullify the power previously granted an authority by statute to sell bonds within a maximum amount sufficient to procure funds to complete its project (*Oklahoma*—50).

Statutes providing for the creation of conservation districts by bond issues and the levying of taxes are constitutional (*Texas*—51). The limitation on state indebtedness does not restrict the issue of bonds for a water conservation system, upon which the state is not liable. A statute authorizing construction of the improvement under the supervision of the state superintendent of public works, and the issue and sale of bonds, is not a violation (*Ohio*—52).

Power conferred on a state water conservation board, on the other hand, to issue coupon bonds without limit as to amount and to run for 40 years violates the constitution where there is no compliance with the constitutional requirements (*Idaho*—53). Proposed contracts under which the state is to give a General State Authority state land upon which to construct water works, with the land and improvement to be leased to the state at an annual rental calculated to pay operating expenses and amortize the bonds, violate the constitution where the bondholders can compel the authority to enforce its agreements with the state (*Pennsylvania*—54).

6. *Miscellaneous Purposes*

A statute creating a General State Authority to which the state will give land on which to construct public projects, to be leased to the state at 10 to 50 percent less than the rentals being paid for the same public purposes, does not violate the constitution. The authority is an independent public corporation; the holders of authority bonds cannot proceed against the lands of the state or the authority; the state can pay the rentals and maintenance expenses upon accrual from current revenues; title to the projects remains in the authority at the end of the contract term, which merely comprises a valid lease agreement and not a sale agreement (*Pennsylvania*—55).

A statutory obligation imposed upon the trustees of an internal improvement fund to pay taxes on swamp and overflow lands granted to the state by Congress, to permit refunding of bond obligations, does not constitute a debt by the state because no obligation is imposed on the state (*Florida*—56). A law appropriating a sum for paying off indebtedness of the state fair is not within the constitutional prohibition because it is for a state institution (*Kentucky*—57).

The Board of Liquidation of the State Debt in one state has been held a department of the state government and not an entity separate from the state. Hence soldier bonus bonds issued by the board under the provisions of a constitutional amendment are bonds of the state (*Louisiana*—58).

C. Revenue Bonds and Special-fund

Since the purpose of a constitutional debt provision is to prevent pledging the revenues of future years, a statute which at the same time it creates a debt creates a fund not otherwise available for general purposes to pay it, is clearly outside the constitutional prohibition (*Colorado*—59).

Obligations of the state or a political subdivision which are not to be a charge on general revenues or pledge the full faith and credit of the state, but are to be paid from designated sources of revenue such as revenues derived from works constructed with the proceeds of the bond issue, do not create debts within the constitutional prohibition (*Indiana*—60, *South Carolina*—61, *Ohio*—62, *Montana*—63). Among the special funds which have been permitted are: revenue derived from utility of a public nature (*West Virginia*—64), special excise taxes (*Alabama*—65), revenue from manufacture and sale of liquor (*Oregon*—66), and railroad rentals (*Georgia*—67).

1. *Transportation*

(A) HIGHWAYS. Generally, the issuance of revenue bonds for highway purposes, payable only out of the motor vehicle fund, the operation of the projects, or highway taxes, is not subject to the constitutional limitation on state debt (*Michigan*—68, *Washington*—69, *Virginia*—70). This is not true in all cases, however.

A statute in one state authorized the sale of state highway debentures in a sum maturing serially at a given rate during a six-year period and made them payable out of a state highway fund into which all moneys received from gasoline license taxes were to be deposited. The law provided that the excise tax was not to be reduced but would remain at the rate fixed until all the debentures were paid. The statute was held unconstitutional as creating a liability within the meaning of the constitution (*Montana*—71).

Another statute authorized the state to borrow money for construction of roads and bridges, issue highway revenue anticipation notes in an aggregate amount not to exceed a specified sum, irrevocably pledge a portion of the gasoline tax, and conditionally pledge a portion of the motor vehicle registration taxes for the payment of the notes. This was held a violation of the constitution insofar as it authorized the issuance of notes and diversion of taxes into a separate fund to pay them and was the creation of state debt (*Oklahoma*—72).

(b) TURNPIKES. The issuance and sale of bonds payable solely from revenues (fares and tolls) derived from a turnpike project, which specifically state on their face that they do not constitute a debt of the state or of any political subdivision or pledge the faith and credit of the state or any political subdivision, does not infringe the constitutional debt limit of the state but creates debt of a separate corporate entity (*Indiana*—73, New *Jersey*—74, *Ohio*—75, *Oklahoma*—76, *Colorado*—77).

(c) BRIDGES. The issuance of revenue bonds for the construction of bridges, to be payable exclusively from tolls and similar charges for the use of the bridges, does not create a general obligation of the state within the constitutional restriction (*Maryland*—78, *Washington*—79, *Nebraska*—80, *California*—81, *Florida*—82). Such arrangements are valid even where they pledge additional sources of revenue such as a portion of gasoline tax receipts (*Florida*—83, *Alabama*—84, *Idaho*—85).

(d) PORTS. A contract between the state department of docks and terminals and a city for the lease of municipal port facilities provided that the money to be paid as rentals would be paid from the first gross operating revenues of the leased facilities. If such revenues were insufficient, the rentals, to the extent of the deficiency, would be payable from gross operating revenue derived from the operation of state-owned terminals at that city and from no other funds. This did not create a "debt" against the state (*Alabama*—86).

A statute authorizing the state to pay from its general funds, under certain conditions, all or part of the annual costs of "maintaining, repairing and operating" the facilities of the state ports authority, a distinct corporate entity having perpetual existence, creates a debt within the meaning of the constitution. The appropriation and allocation of all rentals to be received from the lease of a railroad to a special fund placed at the authority's disposal, to be applied toward payment of refunding bonds, with interest, creates a debt and increases the state's bonded debt (*Georgia*—87).

(E) CANALS. A statute authorizing the issuance of canal certificates to raise money for the completion of certain canals and pledging the surplus revenues of state canals for a prescribed period to the redemption of the certificates creates a debt. This is so even though the law provides that the state will in no wise be bound for payment of the certificates except to the extent of canal revenues for the prescribed period (*New York*—88).

2. *Education*

A bond issue of a state university, payable from university revenues but not from state taxes, does not constitute a debt where no scheme or subterfuge is involved that is intended indirectly to obligate the state to pay out public funds (*Arizona*—89, *Arkansas*—90, *Florida*—91, *Montana*—92). Among the revenue sources that may be validly pledged for payment of university bonds are: income from the university permanent land fund (*Wyoming*—93), dormitory revenues (*Florida*—94, *Kansas*—95, *Minnesota*—96, *Oklahoma*—97, *North Dakota*—98), students' fees and other moneys not derived from state appropriations (*Alabama*—99), income from gifts and bequests (*Montana*—100).

Demonstration School Revenue Certificates, to be issued to supplement an appropriation for construction of a Demonstration School on a state university campus, payable solely from moneys paid to the Board of Control under contract by the Board of Public Instruction of the county for pupil use are not "state bonds" in violation of the constitution (*Florida*—101).

Issuance of bonds by the state board of education to finance the cost of capital outlay projects for school purposes in various counties does not violate the constitution where the bonds are payable solely from motor vehicle license taxes distributable to the counties under a constitutional amendment (The state was not required to pay interest and principal on the bonds if the motor vehicle license tax were insufficient.) (*Florida*—102).

A statute providing for the erection and financing of a student union building at a state university does not create state debt, notwithstanding provisions of the bond resolution and of the loan agreement of the state board of education relative to its furnishing heat, light, power, and water. A branch of the state government which proposes to acquire an additional unit of its plant can pledge the revenues to be derived from the new unit and other units of the plant without creating a state debt (*Montana*—103). A bond issue by the board of trustees of a state college to finance construction of a student union building does not create state debt where the bonds show on their face that they are special obligations payable solely from the revenue to be derived from operation of the union, including the proceeds of a student fee, and are not obligations of the state (*Utah*—104).

A law authorizing the issuance of normal school building bonds and appropriating the permanent school funds to pay them is invalid where the debt limit is reached (*North Dakota*—105). Where a statute provides for the construction of a central building of the state university from the permanent land fund and directs the state land board to convert the fund into cash, the fund is considered an indebtedness of the state in excess of what is allowed under the constitution (*Utah* —106).

A statute authorized the state board of administration to convey to institutional holding associations, for terms not exceeding 50 years, dormitory sites on the campus of any state educational institution. The board would enter into contracts with these associations to lease the dormitories and pay as rental the net income derived from those and other dormitory buildings on the same campus. The money would be used for retiring holding association indebtedness incurred for construction of the buildings. The board could pledge the income for that purpose and enter into any other contract with the association as would be for the best interest of the educational institution affected. This arrangement authorized the creation of state debt contrary to the constitutional provision and was void (*North Dakota*—107).

3. *Public Buildings*

The constitutional debt limitation does not apply to indebtedness incurred in the procurement of property or the erection of buildings or structures for the use of the state, to be paid for wholly out of revenues or income arising from the use or operation of that particular property (*Ohio*—108). This principle has been applied to rents, income, and other revenues of a state tuberculosis sanatorium (*Florida*—109, *Montana*—110), rents and profits of state armory buildings (*Texas*—111, *Kansas*—112), rentals of a state office building (*Florida*—113), rentals, tolls, and charges for the use of public buildings (*Florida*—114).

A similar principle has been applied in the pledging of specific nonbuilding revenues for the construction of buildings. Some examples are: annual tax to be credited to "Prison Building Fund" for new state prison (*Minnesota*—115); $2.50 fee on each civil action filed in state courts to provide funds for capitol addition building (*New Mexico*—116), money in veterans' memorial fund and income from capitol building land grant for construction and furnishing of state building (*Montana*—117).

But the rule seems to be otherwise where additions or improvements are made to state-owned property. If all or part of the revenue from the use of the existing property and the additions or improvements combined is pledged by the state or its board or agency as the sole source of payment of the new construction cost, indebtedness is incurred by the state within the constitutional debt limitation (*Ohio*—118).

A law providing for the erection and operation of a state office building by a state office building commission, for the use and benefit of the state, authorizing the issue of debentures payable from the rentals received from state agencies leasing space, has been held unconstitutional as creating a state debt without electorate approval (*New Mexico*—119). In another state a law for bonding the capitol building lands, the principal payable only from the capitol building fund derived from the sale of the lands, provided for the levy of an annual tax sufficient to meet the interest on the bonds. The bonds, to be deemed a loan from the general fund and to be repaid from the proceeds of sales or leases of capitol building lands, made the statute unconstitutional (*Washington*—120).

4. *Natural Resource Development*

The special-fund doctrine applies to bonds an authority is authorized to issue, payable solely out of a special fund created by revenues from the sale of electric power and water produced by the project and from its properties. (No existing revenues or revenues derived from taxation are pledged directly, indirectly, or contingently.) (*Oklahoma* —121). Similarly, state park improvement bonds issued by the state planning and resources board, expressly providing that they are payable from revenue to be derived from operation of a state park and that they are not indebtedness of the state or of the board, do not constitute debt of the state. Where sufficient money has been placed into a sinking fund to pay outstanding bonded indebtedness of the state, the state planning and resources board can resolve, according to law, to erect improvements in the state park to be paid for from revenues derived from the park. This does not violate the constitutional requirement that all surplus general revenues of the state go into a sinking fund to retire state bonds (*Oklahoma*—122).

5. *Other Purposes*

A statute establishing a state fire and tornado fund to furnish fire and tornado insurance on property of the state, counties, cities, and other political subdivisions does not create indebtedness on the state's part, inasmuch as any claim arising from loss is a claim against the fund alone (*North Dakota*—123).

A statute providing for a bonus to World War II veterans by means of the sale of bonds payable out of a cigarette excise tax under existing and additional statutes does not create a debt against the state (*Washington*—124).

NOTES TO APPENDIX B

1 *Pattison v. Board of Supervisors of Yuba County,* 13 Cal. 175 (1859).
2 *State ex rel. Ach v. Braden,* 125 Ohio St. 307, 181 N.E. 138 (1932).
3 *State v. Raub,* 106 Kan. 196, 186 Pac. 989 (1920).
4 *Martin v. Dade Muck Land Co.,* 95 Fla. 530, 116 So. 449 (1928), appeal dismissed 278 U.S. 560, 49 S. Ct. 25, 73 L. Ed. 505 (1928).
5 *In re Opinion of the Justices,* 237 Ala. 286, 186 So. 485 (1939).
6 *Carlton v. Mathews,* 103 Fla. 301, 137 So. 815 (1931).
7 *Ada County v. Wright,* 60 Ida. 394, 92 P. 2d 134 (1939).
8 *Briggs v. Greenville County,* 137 S.C. 288, 135 S.. 153 1926).
9 *Harris County Flood Control Dist. v. Mann,* 135 Tex. 239, 140 S. W. 2d 1098 (1940).
10 *Kinney v. Astoria,* 108 Ore. 514, 217 Pac. 840 (1923).
11 *Williams v. Town of Dunnellon,* 125 Fla. 114, 169 So. 631 (1936).
12 *Madronah Sales Co. v. Wilburn,* 180 Ga. 837, 181 S.E. 173 (1935).
13 *State v. Florida State Imp. Commission,* 160 Fla. 230, 34 So. 2d 443 (1948).
14 *Crick v. Rash,* 190 Ky. 820, 229 S.W. 63 (1921).
15 *State v. Byrnes,* 219 S.C. 485, 66 S.E. 2d 33 (1951).
16 *State Board of Education v. Aycock,* 198 Ark. 640, 130 S.W. 2d 6 (1939).
17 *Walls v. State Board of Education,* 195 Ark. 955, 116 S.W. 2d 354 (1938).

18 *State v. State Board of Control,* 66 So. 2d 209 (1953).
19 *Lacy v. Fidelity Bank,* 183 N.C. 373, 111 S.E. 612 (1922).
20 *Hinton v. Lacy,* 193 N.C. 496, 137 S.E. 669 (1927).
21 *McMahan v. Olcott,* 65 Ore. 537, 133 Pac. 836 (1913).
22 *Railroad Co. v. Nation,* 82 Kan. 345, 108 Pac. 102 (1910).
23 *University R. Co. v. Holden,* 63 N.C. 410 (1869).
24 *Park v. Candler,* 113 Ga. 647, 39 S.E. 89 (1901), 40 S.E. 523 (1902).
25 *Opinion of the Justices,* 254 Ala. 506, 49 So. 2d 175 (1950); *Norton v. Lusk,* 248 Ala. 110, 26 So. 2d 849 (1946).
26 *State v. Sims,* 134 W. Va. 278, 58 S.E. 2d 766 (1950), rev'd on other grounds in *West Virginia v. Sims,* 341 U.S. 22, 71 S. Ct. 557, 95 L. Ed. 713 (1951).
27 *State v. Mills,* 55 Wis. 229, 12 N.W. 359 (1882).
28 *Long v. Alabama Highway Corp.* 234 Ala. 142, 174 S. 41 (1937).
29 *State ex rel. Syvertson v. Jones,* 74 N.D. 465, 23 N.W. 2d 54 (1946).
30 *Bates v. State Bridge Commission,* 109 W.Va. 186, 153 S.E. 305 (1930).
31 *Rogers v. Garlington,* 284 Ala. 13, 173 So. 372 (1937).
32 *State v. Overseas Road and Toll Bridge Dist.,* 125 Fla. 481, 170 So. 109 (1936).
33 *Highway Com. v. King,* 259 Ky. 414, 82 S.W. 2d 443 (1935).
34 *State v. Regents of University System of Georgia et al.,* 179 Ga. 210, 175 S.E. 567 (1934).
35 *State v. Regents of the University of New Mexico,* 32 N.M. 428, 258 Pac. 571 (1927).
36 *Westbrook v. University of Georgia Athletic Assn., Inc.,* 206 Ga. 667, 58 S.E. 2d 428 (1950).
37 1953 Ops. Atty Gen., No. 51-53, 472.
38 *Bosworth v. State University,* 154 Ky. 370, 157 S.W. 913 (1913).
39 *McClain v. Regents of University,* 124 Ore. 629, 265 Pac. 412 (1928).
40 *James v. State University; James v. The Board of Regents for Eastern Kentcuky State Normal School; James v. Board of Regents for Western Kentucky State Normal School,* 131 Ky. 156, 114 S.W. 767 (1908).
41 *In re Opinion of the Justices,* 252 Ala. 465, 41 So. 2d 761 (1949).
42 *Nordquist v. Ford,* 112 Mont. 278, 114 P. 2d 1071 (1941).
43 *Rutherford v. City of Great Falls,* 107 Mont. 512, 86 P. 2d 656 (1939).
44 *McCutcheon v. State Building Authority,* 13 N.J. 46, 97 A. 2d 663 (1953).
45 1940–1942 Ops. Atty. Gen. 519.
46 *Sholtz v. McCord,* 112 Fla. 248, 150 S. 234 (1933).
47 *Clarke v. South Carolina Public Service Authority,* 177 S.C. 427, 181 S.E. 481 (1935).
48 *Sheldon v. Grand River Dam Authority,* 182 Okla. 24, 76 P. 2d 355 (1938).
49 *State ex rel. Kerr v. Grand River Dam Authority,* 195 Okla. 8, 154 P. 2d 946 (1945).
50 *Wickham v. Grand River Dam Authority,* 189 Okla. 540, 118 P. 2d 640 (1941).
51 *State v. Bank of Mineral Wells,* 251 S.W. 1107 (1923).
52 *Kasch v. Miller,* 104 Ohio St. 281, 135 N.E. 813 (1922).
53 *State Water Conservation Board v. Enking,* 56 Ida. 722, 58 P. 2d 779 (1936).

54 *Kelley v. Earle,* 320 Pa. 449, 182 Atl. 501 (1936); Modified on rehearing 325 Pa. 337, 190 Atl. 140 (1937).
55 *Kelley v. Earle,* 325 Pa. 337, 190 Atl. 140 (1937).
56 *State v. Everglades Drainage Dist.,* 155 Fla. 36, 19 So. 2d 472 (1945).
57 *Rhea v. Newman,* 153 Ky. 604, 156 S.W. 154 (1913).
58 *State ex rel. Kemp v. Board of Liquidation of State Debt,* 214 La. 890, 39 So. 2d 333 (1949).
59 *Watrous v. Golden Chamber of Commerce,* 121 Colo. 521, 218 P. 2d 498 (1950).
60 1946 Ops. Atty. Gen. 43.
61 *Crawford v. Johnson,* 177 S.C. 399,181 S.E. 476 (1935).
62 *Kasch v. Miller,* supra.
63 *State ex rel. Normile v. Cooney,* 100 Mont. 391, 47 P. 2d 637 (1935).
64 *Bates v. State Bridge Comm.,* supra.
65 *Scott v. Alabama Bridge Corp.,* 233 Ala. 12, 169 So. 273 (1936).
66 *Moses v. Meier,* 148 Ore. 185, 35 P. 2d 981 (1934); 1942–1944 Ops Atty. Gen. 222.
67 *Wright v. Hardwick,* 152 Ga. 302, 109 S.E. 903 (1921).
68 *State Highway Commission v. Detroit City Controller,* 331 Mich. 337, 49 N.W. 2d 318 (1951).
69 *State ex rel. Bugge v. Martin,* 38 Wash. 2d 834, 232 P. 2d 833 (1951).
70 *Almond v. Gilmer,* 188 Va. 822, 51 S.E. 2d 272 (1949).
71 *State v. State Highway Comm. et al.,* 89 Mont. 205, 296 Pac. 1033 (1931).
72 *Boswell v. State,* 181 Okla. 435, 74 P. 2d 940 (1937).
73 *Ennis v. State Highway Comm.,* 108 N.E. 2d 687 (1952).
74 *New Jersey Turnpike Authority v. Parsons,* 5 N.J. Super 595, 68 A. 2d 580 (1949) modified 3 N.J. 235, 69 A. 2d 875 (1949).
75 *State ex rel. Allen v. Ferguson,* 155 Ohio St. 26, 97 N.E. 2d 660 (1951).
76 *Application of Oklahoma Turnpike Authority,* 203 Okla. 335, 221 P. 2d 795 (1950).
77 *Watrous v. Golden Chamber of Commerce,* supra.
78 *Wyatt v. State Roads Comm.,* 175 Md. 258, 1 A 2d 619 (1938).
79 *State ex rel. Washington Toll Bridge Authority v. Yelle,* 195 Wash. 636, 82 P. 2d 120 (1938).
80 *Kirby v. Omaha Bridge Commission,* 127 Neb. 382, 255 N.W. 776 (1934).
81 *In re California Toll Bridge Authority,* 212 Cal. 298, 298 Pac. 485 (1931); *California Toll Bridge Authority v. Kelly,* 218 Cal. 7, 21 P. 2d 425 (1933).
82 *State v. Florida State Imp. Commission,* 52 So. 2d 277 (1951).
83 *State v. State Board of Administration,* 157 Fla. 360, 25 So. 2d 880 (1946).
84 *Scott v. Alabama State Bridge Corp.,* supra.
85 *Lyons v. Bottolfsen,* 61 Ida. 281, 101 P. 2d 1 (1940).
86 *Lang v. Mobile (Ala.),* 239 Ala. 331, 195 So. 248 (1940).
87 *State Ports Authority v. Arnall,* 201 Ga. 713, 41 S.E. 2d 246 (1947).
88 *Newell v. People,* 7 N.Y. 9, 13 Bar. 86 (1852).
89 *Board of Regents v. Sullivan,* 45 Ariz. 245, 42 P. 2d 619 (1935).
90 *Jacobs v. Sharp,* 211 Ark. 865, 202 S.W. 2d 964 (1947).
91 *Hopkins v. Baldwin,* 123 Fla. 649, 167 So. 677 (1936).

92   *State v. State Board of Education et al.,* 97 Mont. 371, 34 P. 2d 515 (1934).
93   *Arnold v. Bond,* 47 Wyo. 236, 34 P. 2d 28 (1934).
94   *State v. Board of Control,* supra.
95   *State ex rel. Fatzer v. Board of Regents,* 167 Kan. 587, 207 P. 2d 373 (1949).
96   *Fanning v. University of Minnesota,* 183 Minn. 222, 236 N.W. 217 (1931).
97   *Application of Board of Regents of Okla. College for Women,* 204 Okla. 385, 230 P. 2d 453 (1951); *Application of Board of Regents for Okla. Agr. and Mechanical Colleges,* 196 Okla. 622, 167 P. 2d 883 (1946); *Application of Board of Regents of University of Okla.,* 195 Okla. 641, 161 P. 2d 447 (1945); *Baker v. Carter.* 165 Okla. 116, 25 P. 2d 747 (1933).
98   *State ex rel. Kaufman v. Davis,* 59 N.D. 191, 229 N.W. 105 (1930).
99   *Harman v. Alabama College,* 235 Ala. 148, 177 So. 747 (1937).
100 *Barbour v. State Board of Education,* 92 Mont. 321, 13 P. 2d 225 (1932).
101 *State v. Board of Control,* 65 So. 2d 469 (1953).
102 *State v. Board of Education of Florida,* 67 So. 2d 627 (1953).
103 *State v. State Board of Education et al.,* 97 Mont. 121, 33 P. 2d 516 (1934).
104 *Spence v. Utah State Agricultural College,* 225 P. 2d 18 (1950).
105 *State ex rel. University & School Lands v. McMillan,* 12 N.D. 280, 96 N.W. 310 (1903).
106 *State ex rel. University of Utah v. Candland,* 36 Utah 406, 104 Pac. 285 (1909).
107 *Wilder v. Murphy,* 56 N.D. 436, 218 N.W. 156 (1928).
108 *State ex rel. Public Institutional Bldg. Authority v. Griffith,* 135 Ohio St. 604, 22 N.E. 2d 200 (1939).
109 *Brash v. State Tuberculosis Board,* 124 Fla. 652, 169 So. 218 (1936)
110 *State ex rel. Hawkins v. State Board of Examiners et al.,* 97 Mont. 441, 35 P. 2d 116 (1934).
111 *Texas National Guard Armory Board v. McGraw,* 132 Tex. 613, 126 S.W. 2d 627 (1939).
112 *State ex rel. Fatzer v. Armory Board et al.,* 174 Kan. 369, 256 P. 2d 143 (1953).
113 *State v. Florida State Imp. Commission,* 158 Fla. 743, 30 So. 2d 97 (1947).
114 *State ex rel. Watson v. Caldwell,* 156 Fla. 618, 23 So. 2d 855 (1945), supplemented 24 So. 2d 797 (1946).
115 *Brown v. Ringdahl,* 109 Minn. 6, 122 N.W. 469 (1909).
116 *State ex rel. Capitol Addition Bldg. Comm. v. Connelly,* 39 N.M. 312, 46 P. 2d 1097 (1935).
117 *Willett v. State Board of Examiners,* 112 Mont. 317, 115 P. 2d 287 (1941).
118 *State ex rel. Public Institutional Bldg. Authority v. Griffith,* supra.
119 *State Office Building Comm. v. Trujillo,* 46 N.M. 29, 120 P. 2d 434 (1941); *Byrant v. State Office Building Comm.,* 46 N.M. 58, 120 P. 2d 452 (1941).

120   *State ex rel. State Capitol Commission v. Lister,* 91 Wash. 9, 156 Pac.
      858 (1916).
121   *Sheldon v. Grand River Dam Authority,* supra.
122   *Application of Oklahoma Planning and Resources Board,* 201 Okla.
      178, 203 P. 2d 415 (1949).
123   *Minot Special School Dist. No. 1 v. Olsness,* 53 N.D. 683, 208 N.W.
      968, 45 A.L.R. 1337 (1926).
124   *Gruen v. Tax Commission et al.,* 35 Wash 2d 1, 211 P. 2d 651 (1949).

Notes

CHAPTER 1

1   See B. U. Ratchford, *American State Debts* (Durham: Duke University Press, 1941), chaps. 2 and 3, for a detailed coverage of state borrowing prior to 1820.
2   Reginald C. McGrane, *Foreign Bondholders and American State Debts* (New York: The Macmillan Co., 1935), p. 5.
3   For an analysis of why these activities were carried on by state governments rather than by private enterprise, see Horace Secrist, *An Economic Analysis of the Constitutional Restrictions Upon Public Indebtedness in the United States* (Madison: University of Wisconsin Press, 1914), pp. 16–17.
4   See McGrane, *Foreign Bondholders* . . . , p. 6, for a general discussion, and chaps. VII and IX–XII for references to specific states.
5   McGrane, *Foreign Bondholders* . . . , p. 9.
6   R. C. McGrane, *The Panic of 1837* (Chicago: University of Chicago Press, 1924); D. R. Dewey, *Financial History of the United States* (New York: Longmans, Green & Co., 1939); and many others.
7   See McGrane, *Foreign Bondholders* . . . , for a complete treatment of the relations between American states and foreign investors in the face of defaults and later repudiations.
8   Ratchford, *American State Debts*, pp. 100–104.
9   Ratchford, p. 114.
10 Ratchford, pp. 116–20.
11 *Rhode Island Constitution*, 1843, art. IV, sec. 13.
12 *New Jersey Constitution*, 1844, art. IV, sec. 13.
13 Because of their very recent statehood, data relating to Alaska and Hawaii could not be included in this study beyond a reference to their constitutional provisions in this chapter.

CHAPTER 2

1   Wylie Kilpatrick, *Financing State and Local Government in Florida* (Tallahassee: Florida Citizens Tax Council, 1957), p. 86.
2   Lawrence S. Knappen, *Revenue Bonds and the Investor* (New

137

York: Prentice-Hall, 1939); Jerome J. Shestack, "The Public Authority," 105 *Pennsylvania Law Review* 533 (1957); Jon Magnusson, "Lease Financing by Municipal Corporations as a Way Around Debt Limitations," 25 *George Washington Law Review* 377 (1956-1957); and many others.

3   Knappen, *Revenue Bonds . . .* , p. 1.
4   Also see E. H. Foley, "Revenue Financing of Public Enterprises," 35 *Michigan Law Review* 1 (1936); Jefferson B. Fordham, "Revenue Bond Sanctions," 42 *Columbia Law Review* 395 (1942); Knappen, *Revenue Bonds . . .* , chaps. I–III; R. F. Mooney, "Tax Supported Revenue Bonds: A Study of Methods Used to Avoid Constitutional Limitations on Public Debt," *Association of Life Insurance Council, Proceedings,* 1957; and Ratchford, *American State Debts,* Ch. XVIII.
5   *In re Canal Certificates,* 19 Colo. 63 (1889).
6   *Newell v. People,* 7 N. Y. 9, 12 (1852).
7   *State v. Moorer,* 152 S. C. 455, 491 (1929).
8   See Ratchford, *American State Debts,* chap. XVIII, for a more detailed history of the development of the special-fund doctrine.
9   Shestack, "The Public Authority," p. 559.
10 Mortimer S. Edelstein, "The Authority Plan—Tool of Modern Government," *The Cornell Law Quarterly,* vol. XXVIII (1942–1943). Here three reasons for the establishment of an authority are noted: (1) to avoid debt limits; (2) to close a jurisdictional gap, i.e., to operate a public project in two or more political units; and (3) to permit public use of functional lines of business without the profit motive. In Council of State Governments, *Public Authorities in the States* (Chicago: Council of State Governments, 1953), eight reasons are noted, but for the most part they may be condensed into the three noted above.
11 Knappen, *Revenue Bonds . . .* , chap. IX.
12 See Frederick Bird, *A Study of the New York Port Authority* (New York: Dun & Bradstreet, 1949), and E. W. Bard, *The Port of New York Authority* (New York: Columbia University Press, 1939), for a history of its development.
13 The Pennsylvania Turnpike Commission and the Washington Toll Bridge Authority among others.
14 This last item makes information on some authorities difficult to obtain. As a classic example, when, during another study, a request was made of state governors to obtain the identity of public authorities in the states, one governor (of a state unnamed for

obvious reasons) replied that no one seemed to know because the authorities apparently had no reports to make, and it would take a couple of months to find out what state authorities were in fact operating.

15 *Public Authorities in the States.*

16 *State v. McCauley,* 15 Calif. 429, 455 (1860).

17 For example, such a program in Wisconsin for construction of an addition to the state office building was declared unconstitutional in 1954 because state-owned land was mortgaged. When the mortgage provision was changed in 1955, the court approved. *State v. Giessel,* first case 267 Wis. 331 (1954), second case 271 Wis. 15 (1955).

18 Mooney calls them tax supported revenue bonds as differentiated from revenue bonds for toll roads, dormitories, and other self-liquidating projects, because the rental revenue servicing the debt comes from the general fund of the state or local unit leasing the building.

19 See *Moody's Municipal and Government Manual,* 1961, pp. 406–15 for a description of the Florida technique.

20 Among others, see Eugene C. Lee, "Use of Lease-Purchase Agreements to Finance Capital Improvements," *Municipal Finance,* vol. XXIV (Nov. 1951), and Edward P. Riehl, "Lease-Purchase Contracts for Public Property," *Municipal Finance,* vol. XXV (Aug. 1952), for a more complete description of the lease-purchase method of financing public improvements.

21 Ratchford, *American State Debts,* chap. XI, has a description of the reimbursement techniques as used in the various states. Wisconsin's use of this technique can best be described by a quote from *The Wisconsin Taxpayer,* vol. 23, no. 2 (Nov. 15, 1955): "County highway debt consists of two types: borrowing for purposes of the county trunk highway system and borrowing for the state trunk highway system. Debt for county highway purposes, like other local full faith and credit debt, is paid for by a property tax levy. The bonds for state trunk highway purposes, however, must be approved by the state highway commission before issuance, and are retired with state funds derived from gasoline and other state highway users taxes. The county pays the interest on these bonds from its own funds. In effect, the state has a statutory, a political and a moral obligation to pay the principal on these state highway system bonds even though they constitute a legal county obligation."

22 Reimbursement obligations are generally not included in published state debt figures.

23 The debts of the Port of New York Authority and other interstate and international authorities are not included. Because of the obvious use of the authority device as a jurisdictional measure in those cases, their debts will not be considered a part of state debt. The Bureau of the Census justifies this exclusion on the same grounds.

24 Even so these figures do not include debts for all toll roads. Omitted are the bonds of toll roads operated by the state highway departments in Colorado, Connecticut, and New Hampshire (some of these bonds are revenue bonds and are included in Table 7); and part of the toll road debt of New York and New Jersey authorities for which the full faith and credit of those states has been pledged.

25 Peter R. Nehemkis, Jr., "The Public Authority: Some Legal and Practical Aspects," 47 *Yale Law Journal* 14 (1937), pp. 26–29.

26 Ratchford, *American State Debts,* p. 517.

27 Richard K. Stuart, *Financing Public Improvements by the State of Maine* (Augusta: University of Maine Press, 1957), p. 141.

CHAPTER 3

1 *Public Authorities in the States,* p. 17.

2 These restrictions apply to full-faith and credit borrowing only. Nonguaranteed borrowing is exempt from the restrictions.

3 B. U. Ratchford, "State and Local Debt Limitations," *National Tax Association, Proceedings,* 1958. Ratchford's results were slightly different than the results shown in Table 9 because he had to use population and personal income figures for 1956. The results in Table 9 are based upon 1957 population and personal income figures. The differences are small, however, and inconsequential to the analysis.

CHAPTER 4

1 *Public Authorities in the States,* Appendix B, table 7; B. U. Ratchford, "New Forms of State Debts," *Southern Economic Journal,* vol. VIII (1941–1942); Ratchford, *American State Debts;* Wisconsin Executive Office, *Public Debt,* Nov. 1, 1959; and others.

2 See the Technical Note to this chapter.

3 The nature of revenue bonds as callable or not callable is ap-

parently not significant as a determinant of the interest cost on revenue bonds. See the Technical Note to this chapter.

4 It is estimated that New York saved $120 million in interest payments when it pledged the credit of the state on the bonds of the New York State Thruway Authority. E. B. Isaak, "Economic Feasibility of the New York State Thruway," *Civil Engineering* (Nov. 1953), p. 36.

5 *Public Authorities in the States,* Appendix B, table VII.

6 Linearity of the yield curve is not an unreasonable assumption here and in equation (4), because this model is concerned with bonds whose maturities exceed five years. For maturities less than five years the model would probably give unreliable results, inasmuch as the yield curve is clearly nonlinear over a range of maturities from zero to five years.

CHAPTER 5

1 Marshall E. Dimock, "Government Corporations: a Focus of Policy and Administration," *American Political Science Review,* vol. VIII (1949); Herman Prichett, "The Paradox of the Government Corporation," *Public Administration Review,* vol. II (1941–1942).

2 Harold Seidman, "The Theory of the Autonomous Government Corporation: A Critical Appraisal," *Public Administration Review,* vol. XI (1952).

3 Charles W. Ingler, "Are Public Controls over Authorities Adequate?" *National Tax Association, Proceedings,* 1957, pp. 261–62.

4 J. R. Rothermel, Jr., "Memorandum to Subcommittee on Revision of Article 8: Constitutional Revision Commission," Madison, Wisconsin, August 11, 1960 (typewritten).

5 Rothermel, p. 7.

6 *Public Authorities in the States,* p. 85.

7 *Public Authorities in the States,* Appendix B, table X.

8 *Business Week,* February 6, 1960, p. 107.

9 P. 108.

10 State of New York, Temporary Commission on Coordination on State Activities, *Public Authorities under New York State,* Legislative Document No. 46 (Albany: Williams Press, 1956), p. 450.

11 P. 447.

12 P. 451.

13 P. 452.

CHAPTER 6

1 The New York State Thruway Authority and the New Jersey Highway Authority have issued bonds for which the credit of their respective states has been pledged.

2 B. U. Ratchford, "A Formula for Limiting State and Local Debts," *Quarterly Journal of Economics,* vol. LI (1936–1937). Ratchford suggests that the best measure for this purpose would be average revenue of the state government.

3 Stuart, *Financing Public Improvements,* p. 137.

4 Kentucky Legislative Research Commission, *Debt Administration,* Research Publication 30 (Frankfurt, 1952).

5 The Tax Foundation, Inc., *Constitutional Debt Control in the States,* Project Note No. 35 (New York: by the Tax Foundation, Inc., 1954). The Tax Foundation is perhaps the foremost exponent of this group.

Bibliography

PUBLIC DOCUMENTS

Kentucky Legislative Research Commission. *Debt Administration.* Research Publication 30. February, 1952.

State of California, Assembly Interim Committee on Finance and Insurance. *A Research Report on Public Works Financing.* 1952.

State of New Jersey, The Governors Committee on Preparatory Research for the New Jersey Constitutional Convention. *Constitutional Limitations on the Creation of Debt.* May, 1947.

State of New York, Temporary State Commission on Coordination of State Activities. *Public Authorities under New York State. Legislative Document No. 46.* Albany: Williams Press, 1956.

U.S. Bureau of the Census. *Compendium of State Government Finances 1920–1959.*

———. *Census of Governments:* 1957. Vol. III, Nos. 1–5.

U.S. Bureau of Public Roads. *Highway Statistics.* 1946–1958.

U.S. Department of Commerce. *Progress and Feasibility of Toll Roads and Their Relation to the Federal Aid Program.* 1955.

U.S. Inter-Agency Committee on Water Resources. *Proposed Practices for Economic Analysis of River Basin Projects,* revised. Prepared by the Subcommittee on Evaluation Standards, 1958.

Wisconsin Executive Office, *Public Debt,* Nov. 1, 1959.

BOOKS AND PAMPHLETS

American Petroleum Industries. *Toll Road Facts.* New York: by the American Petroleum Industries, 1955.

Bard, E. W. *The Port of New York Authority.* New York: Columbia University Press, 1939.

Bird, Frederick L. *Revenue Bonds.* Los Angeles: The Haynes Foundation, 1941.

———. *A Study of the New York Port Authority.* New York: Dun & Bradstreet, 1949.

Bollens, John C. *Special District Government in the United States.* Berkeley: University of California Press, 1957.

Bowen, Howard R. *Toward Social Economy.* New York: Rinehart & Company, 1948.

143

Chernak, Lawrence E. *The Law of Revenue Bonds.* Washington: National Institute of Municipal Law Officers, 1954.

The Council of State Governments. *Public Authorities in the States.* Chicago: by the Council of State Governments, 1953.

Dewey, D. R. *Financial History of the United States,* 12th ed., revised. New York: Longmans, Green & Company, 1939.

Eckstein, Otto. *Water Resource Development: The Economics of Project Evaluation.* Cambridge: Harvard University Press, 1958.

Fowler, John F., Jr. *Revenue Bonds.* New York: Harper Brothers, 1938.

Friedman, W., ed. *The Public Corporation.* London: Stevens and Sons, 1934.

The Institute of Transportation and Traffic Engineering. *Toll-Road Developments and Their Significance in the Provision of Expressways.* Berkeley: University of California, 1953.

Kilpatrick, Wylie. *Financing State and Local Governments in Florida.* Tallahassee: Florida Citizens Tax Council, 1957.

Knappen, L. S. *Revenue Bonds and the Investor.* New York: Prentice-Hall, 1939.

Krutilla, J. V., and Eckstein, Otto. *Multiple Purpose River Development: Studies in Applied Economic Analysis.* Baltimore: Resources for the Future, Inc., 1958.

Lindman, Bertrand H. *Supplemental Bond Financing for the Acceleration of the Ohio Highway Program.* March 14, 1951.

McCarty, John F. *Highway Financing by the Toll System.* Berkeley: Bureau of Public Administration, University of California, 1951.

McKean, Roland N. *Efficiency in Government Through Systems Analysis.* A Rand Corporation Research Study. New York: John Wiley & Sons, 1958.

McGrane, Reginald C. *Foreign Bondholders and American State Debts.* New York: The Macmillan Company, 1935.

———. *The Panic of 1837.* Chicago: The University of Chicago Press, 1924.

Moody's Manual of Government Securities.

New Jersey State Chamber of Commerce. *Government by "Authorities" for New Jersey.* Newark: by the New Jersey State Chamber of Commerce, 1952.

Pennsylvania State Chamber of Commerce. *The State "Authority" Programs.* State Affairs Bulletin No. 3. Harrisburg: by the Pennsylvania State Chamber of Commerce, 1951.

Pigou, A. C. *The Economics of Welfare,* 4th ed., revised. London: Macmillan & Company, 1932.

Ratchford, B. U. *American State Debts*. Durham: Duke University Press, 1941.

Secrist, Horace. *An Economic Analysis of the Constitutional Restrictions upon Public Indebtedness in the United States*. Madison: University of Wisconsin Press, 1914.

Smithies, Arthur. *The Budgetary Process in the United States*. New York: McGraw-Hill, 1955.

Stuart, Roland K. *Financing Public Improvements by the State of Maine*. Augusta: University of Maine Press, 1957.

The Tax Foundation, Inc. *Constitutional Debt Control in the States*. Project Note No. 35. New York: by the Tax Foundation, Inc., 1954.

———. *Controlling Government Corporations*. Project Note No. 37. New York: by the Tax Foundation, Inc., 1955.

Trull, Edna. *Resources and Debts of the Forty-Eight States*. New York: Dun & Bradstreet, 1937.

ARTICLES AND PERIODICALS

Adsit, Ted B. "The Lease-Purchase Financing Method." *Public Management,* Vol. XXXVIII (1956).

Business Week (February 6, 1960).

Dimock, Marshall E. "Government Corporations: a Focus of Policy and Administration." *Public Administration Review,* Vol. VIII (1949).

Edelstein, Mortimer S. "The Authority Plan—Tool of Modern Government." *The Cornell Law Quarterly,* Vol. XXVIII (1942–1943).

Foley, E. H. "Revenue Financing of Public Enterprises." 35 *Michigan Law Review* 1 (1936–1937).

Fordham, Jefferson B. "Revenue Bond Sanctions." 42 *Columbia Law Review* 395 (1942).

Gerwig, Robert. "Public Authorities: Legislative Panacea?" *Journal of Public Law,* Vol. 5, No. 2 (1956).

Gulick, Luther. " 'Authorities' and How to Use Them." *The Tax Review,* Vol. VIII, No. 11 (1947).

Hirshleifer, J. "On the Theory of Optimal Investment Decisions." *Journal of Political Economy,* Vol. LXVI (1958).

Isaak, E. R. "Economic Feasibility of the New York State Thruway." *Civil Engineering* (November, 1953).

Ingler, Charles W. "Are Public Controls over Authorities Adequate?" *National Tax Association, Proceedings* (1957).

Lee, Eugene C. "Use of Lease-Purchase Agreements to Finance Capital Improvements." *Municipal Finance,* Vol. XXIV (1951–1952).

Magnusson, Jon. "Lease Financing by Municipal Corporations as a

Way Around Debt Limitations." 25 *George Washington Law Review* 377 (1956–1957).

Margolis, Julius. "An Evaluation of Water Resource Development." *American Economic Review,* Vol. XLIX, No. 1 (1959).

Mooney, R. F. "Tax Supported Revenue Bonds: A Study of Methods Used to Avoid Constitutional Limitations on Public Debt." *Association of Life Insurance Council, Proceedings* (1957).

Nehemkis, Peter R., Jr. "The Public Authority: Some Legal and Practical Aspects." 47 *Yale Law Review* 14 (1937).

Prichett, Herman. "The Paradox of the Government Corporation." *Public Administration Review,* Vol. II (1941–1942).

Ratchford, B. U. "A Formula for Limiting State and Local Debts." *Quarterly Journal of Economics,* Vol. LI (1936–1937).

———. "New Forms of State Debt." *Southern Economic Journal,* Vol. VIII (1941–1942).

———. "State and Local Debt Limitations." *National Tax Association, Proceedings* (1958).

Seidman, Harold. "The Theory of the Autonomous Government Corporation: A Critical Appraisal." *Public Administration Review,* Vol. XI (1952).

Shestack, Jerome J. "The Public Authority." 105 *Pennsylvania Law Review* 533 (1957).

Steiner, Gilbert Y. "A State Building Authority: Solution to Construction Needs?" *Current Economic Comment,* Vol. XVII (1955).

Trimble, John T. "Public Revenue Bonds." *Municipal Finance,* Vol. XXV (1952–1953).

Walker, Mabel. "The Authority Device for Financing Public Works." *Tax Policy,* Vol. XXV, No. 12 (1958).

The Wisconsin Taxpayer, Vol. 23, No. 2, Madison: The Wisconsin Taxpayers Alliance (1955).

Wood, David M. "Current Poblems Affecting Authority Financing." *Municipal Finance,* Vol. XXVIII (1955).

———. "Special Authorities." *Municipal Finance,* Vol. XXV (1952–1953).

UNPUBLISHED

The Council of State Governments. Files on study of public authorities.

Rothermel, J. R., Jr. "Memorandum to Subcommittee on Revision of Article 8: Constitution Revision Commission." Madison, Wisconsin, 1960 (typewritten).

———. "The Wisconsin State Building Program: A Study in Adminis-
trative Responsibility." Unpublished masters thesis, Department of
Political Science, University of Minnesota, 1958.
U.S. Bureau of the Census. Files on state debts.

OTHER SOURCES

Madison Wisconsin. A survey of state authorities as to nature of
operation, structure, source of revenues, outstanding debts, insurance practices, and other data.
Madison, Wisconsin. Survey of state investment funds as to holdings
of own state securities.

Index

149